PRAISE FOR PICTURE YOURSELF A LEADER

Picture Yourself a Leader is a creatively written guide full of bite-sized morsels that provide nourishment and support for newcomers to continuous improvement, change management, and problem solving—and for experienced leaders. Individuals can read the book (or jump around to the tidbit you need at the moment), and it's also well suited for teams and book club discussions. Elisabeth Swan shares her thoughts and experiences (along with her own illustrations) with humor and jargon-free clarity. She also deftly incorporates "wisdom of the crowd" nuggets from others in her professional circles. Picture yourself... a reader of this book!

— MARK GRABAN, AUTHOR OF BOOKS
INCLUDING *THE MISTAKES THAT MAKE US*

This gem offers a well-written and a refreshing take on leadership, problem solving, and the relationship between the two. Elisabeth nails the most common mindsets and behaviors that get in peoples' way and offers practical and inviting ways to explore alternatives. Shifting how we think and act results in better problem solving and leaders that people truly want to follow.

— KAREN MARTIN, AUTHOR OF *CLARIFY FIRST*

In *Picture Yourself a Leader*, author Elisabeth Swan offers big leadership lessons in small bites and sprinkles them with seasoning from some of the world's best leadership thinkers. Read it through and then keep it nearby for instant lessons when you're looking for a breakthrough idea on an important topic. Like daily exercise, you will improve your leadership shape faster than you thought possible!

— RICHARD SHERIDAN, CEO & CHIEF STORYTELLER AT MENLO INNOVATIONS, AND AUTHOR OF *JOY INC.* AND *CHIEF JOY OFFICER*

Elisabeth Swan, based on her vast experience working with organizations to help them grow exceptional leaders, gives us 50 micro-lessons that can help us navigate through the trials and tribulations of leadership. Each is brief, illustrated through real-life stories, and given a catchy title easy to relate to like "Rise, Shine, and Make it Worthwhile" and "Let Ink Make You Think." The book is full of wisdom, learned the hard way, by living through and learning to overcome these "potholes." How can you use them? First, don't try to memorize them then call them up for every encounter as a leader. Do try to use them in your deliberate practice. Deliberate practice means you have something specific to practice, you have a picture of what the ideal state looks like, and you try out the behavior repeatedly, working to close the gap between ideal and actual. Pick one or two at a time to practice. Even better do it with a companion so you can coach each other... and you will feel your leadership grow.

— JEFFREY LIKER, BESTSELLING AUTHOR OF *THE TOYOTA WAY*

Elisabeth Swan has crafted an insightful and delightful book to help leaders of all kinds become more effective as they work to create change. The illustrations—coupled with stories, reflections, and tips—highlight the challenges we all inevitably face when leading change and solving problems. Each chapter includes prompts to help readers experiment with how to make their way forward as they learn from failure and success. If you are looking to become a better problem solver, leader, or human being, *Picture Yourself a Leader* is your guide to help you on your journey!

— KATIE ANDERSON, AUTHOR OF *LEARNING TO LEAD, LEADING TO LEARN*

I like the light perspective Elisabeth takes when writing. The stories, illustrations, and analogies were so close to my day-to-day reality, that it is impossible not to relate them to our lives. I could visually see her and her husband rushing for a Harvard play, genius. I could imagine episodes happening in front of me. I was truly captivated by this book.

— SAMMY OBARA, CEO OF HONSHA.ORG

Elisabeth brings unique, insightful, and entertaining guidance to anyone looking for practical ways to improve how they think and act—in both professional and personal contexts. This is a refreshing and comprehensive look at good habits, bad habits, and ways to manage both. Worthwhile for current and future leaders.

— PETE PANDE, AUTHOR OF *THE SIX SIGMA WAY*

This is a wonderful book. William Morris, a British Textile Designer and poet, said that you should "have nothing in your houses that you do not know to be beautiful or believe to be useful." I apply this rule very strictly to my book collection. If a book is not nice to look at, or useful for my work or my development, then I will not grant it a place on my bookshelf. This book fulfills both those criteria. It is a brilliant collection of beautiful illustrations and thought-provoking stories which together prompt reflection and deep thinking. The addition of the 'Wisdom of the Crowd' after every story gives extra colour with multiple perspectives and examples—further expanding the story. The prompts to capture your thoughts and ideas, in your own words (or maybe your own doodles?), takes the reflection to another level. Anyone in a leadership position (or anyone wanting to be) would find this book useful for sparking thought and conversation, and for helping them work and play more effectively with their colleagues."

— GEMMA JONES, IMPROVEMENT COACH AND
FOUNDER OF SPARK IMPROVEMENT, LTD.

As with her first book, *The Problem-Solver's Toolkit*, Elisabeth provides tangible, bite-sized takeaways that problem solvers, established leaders, and people discovering their influence will appreciate. Having worked within the University of California's continuing education division for 15+ years, it's clear that effective leadership is in higher demand than ever before. We look forward to introducing *Picture Yourself a Leader* to students pursuing Lean Six Sigma training at UC San Diego.

— ANGELA MILLER, PROGRAM MANAGER FOR UC
SAN DIEGO DIVISION OF EXTENDED STUDIES

I love how Elisabeth Swan so effectively imparts the "wisdom of many" in her book *Picture Yourself a Leader*. The book is elegantly written, in a single-point lesson format. Stories, both hers as well as those of countless others, are integrated throughout and effectively drive home the message. Each of the topics is succinctly delivered, reinforced by the experiences of colleagues—and followed up with a summary and prompts on how to relate the lesson to your situation. *Picture Yourself a Leader* is an invaluable resource for those seeking to improve at work, in the community, or in their personal life.

— MIKE OSTERLING, CO-AUTHOR OF SEVERAL
BOOKS INCLUDING *VALUE STREAM MAPPING* AND
THE KAIZEN EVENT PLANNER

A brilliant collection of stories that addresses the people-centric challenges we've all experienced at one time or another. Elisabeth's storytelling resonates on so many levels and makes the topics easy to navigate and read while providing insight and reflection along the way. I appreciate how the book is not necessarily designed to be read from front to back. It can be used for weekly learning (like a skill-a-week calendar), or you can turn to the topic that is most pressing. The combination of illustrations, stories, crowd-sourced ideas, and questions allows the individual to connect with each topic in unique ways, allowing for deeper discovery and reflection along the way. Unlike other leadership books, this one will stay within hands reach, because when we hit the inevitable snag, we can flip through the pages for guidance and a little company.

— JENNIFER AYERS, EXECUTIVE DIRECTOR AT
NORTHWEST HIGH PERFORMANCE ENTERPRISE
CONSORTIUM (NWHPEC)

Really excellent job. Very few books on management & leadership have the joy, zest, and smarts that *Picture Yourself a Leader* does. Elisabeth has written this for more people than the professional striver. It's really fun to read—I laughed out loud—it's accessible and enlightening to boot. I plan on buying this book for my daughters, and for myself. I found it incredibly valuable.

— BRIAN MANNING, FORMER EDITOR AT THE
INTERNATIONAL HERALD TRIBUNE IN PARIS

An engaging and practical guide for problem solvers and leaders, loaded with helpful insights. With the warmth and steadiness of a supportive coach, Elisabeth Swan walks readers through stories that make you think, and she serves up wisdom you can apply in your own journey. The inventive format makes it easy to learn and apply new ideas quickly. As a bonus, chapters can easily be utilized to jump start conversations in team meetings on issues leaders face every day—I am looking forward to sharing a lesson at our next meeting!

— KATE PARMELEE, DIRECTOR OF STRATEGIC
INITIATIVES & INNOVATION FOR THE CITY OF
PORT ST. LUCIE

Picture Yourself a Leader puts the reader at the center of their own journey to navigating change. Drawing on three decades of research, coaching, improv, teaching, and consulting, Elisabeth Swan builds a guidebook to holistic leadership that delights, surprises, and inspires.

— LAURA ORLANDO, ADJUNCT PROFESSOR AT
BOSTON UNIVERSITY

Picture Yourself a Leader is a fantastic guide for anyone interested in improving their ability to lead with humility and curiosity while becoming more adept at guiding problem solvers. The book is filled with memorable stories that illustrate the lessons we all need to learn or be reminded of regularly and is filled with quotes from some of my favorite authors and thought leaders. You can benefit from this book if you are a new beginner or a seasoned professional and will enjoy the humor and humanity with each page turn.

— CHRIS BURNHAM, HOST OF *THE LEAN LEADERSHIP* PODCAST

This book should be in every leader's briefcase—or backpack or purse—while each of Elisabeth Swan's lessons from her leadership journey takes only a few minutes to read, the learnings are deep and deeply useful. And the illustrations rock!

— BELLA ENGLEBACH, AUTHOR OF *CREATIVELY LEAN,* AND HOST OF *THE EDGES OF LEAN* PODCAST

Elisabeth Swan tells great stories that bring to life the challenges faced by anyone trying to improve their work. She gently guides us with insights from her own rich experience and pulls in wisdom from many others who devote their lives to continuous improvement. For each challenge, she prompts us to consider what specific steps we might take. If you are looking for a volume that will give you food for thought and reflection or are looking for encouragement that this work does make a difference, this is a wonderful resource.

— HUGH ALLEY, AUTHOR OF *BECOMING THE SUPERVISOR*

Picture Yourself a Leader made me burst out laughing and provoked some serious reflection. As a department head in the ever-changing film and television business, I am always looking for better ways to communicate with my colleagues. Elisabeth's relatable stories, quotes, and amusing drawings illustrate novel tactics to improve relationships and embrace change while promoting empathy and camaraderie. Her humor and writing style make for a warm, easy read but don't be fooled by its accessibility. These topics resonate long after reading. Her positive intelligence is inspiring. Bravo!!

— ANNE MCCABE, DIRECTOR OF *IDINA MENZEL: WHICH WAY TO THE STAGE?*

This book is an indispensable resource for any leader. It provides practical solutions to the myriad of challenges leaders face on a regular basis. What I love most about the book is it points out how things can go wrong, even when you think you're doing it right. The illustrations, stories, and crowd-sourced advice make this a quick and entertaining read.

— JEFF TOISTER, AUTHOR OF *THE SERVICE CULTURE HANDBOOK*

If you want to become a better problem solver, if you're concerned with your career progression, this book will guide you to not only solve departmental challenges but also how to gain insights into your own path to success. It will help you become a better leader and coach to your teams. It will help you find solutions and improvements with greater focus and speed. A must-read for anyone interested in becoming a leader worth following.

— SASHA YABLONOVSKY, CO-CEO OF LOANSPARK

The unique format of *Picture Yourself a Leader* lends itself to exploring important people-centric leadership concepts that many books miss or bury. The topics aren't presented in a prescriptive style, but instead invite you to reflect on each concept to determine if they add value to you and your organization.

— KEVIN MEYER, CO-FOUNDER OF GEMBA
ACADEMY

Each chapter of *Picture Yourself a Leader* will motivate and encourage you. This distinctive collection of sketches and management wisdom delivers invaluable guidance on how to work with other people, manage change more effectively, and lead with confidence. Use it as a resource to experiment with new habits and become a better steward of your own influence. This candid, humorous, and charming book is essential reading.

— *SABIHA MUMTAZ, ASSISTANT PROFESSOR AT*
UNIVERSITY OF WOLLONGONG IN DUBAI

I got my copy of *Picture Yourself a Leader*, and *I could not stop* until I'd read it cover to cover. I had so many moments where I couldn't stop laughing and nodding as I recognized the reality we live in every day! Elisabeth puts a much needed sense of humor into what truly happens during Lean process improvement. This is a must-read for anyone looking to transform the culture and develop the "Lean muscles" of those who do the work. You'll find yourself making a huge leap forward as a trainer, mentor, and leader that people want to follow.

— LILY ANGELOCCI, LEAN SIX SIGMA MASTER
BLACK BELT AND TRANSFORMATIONAL
HEALTHCARE LEAD FOR UC SAN DIEGO HEALTH

Picture Yourself a Leader is an open invitation to discover how you influence others—in *all* the ways—as a parent, friend, colleague, teacher, professional leader, or ordinary citizen. You'll be surprised! Elisabeth Swan is a sharpshooter at stirring things up—deep, hilarious, and on target. Her anecdotes and stories bring it home and let it resonate. Swan is so adept that it's more like listening than reading. You can cherrypick stories depending on the issue at hand and test out new behaviors. It's a reference book you can leave around indefinitely just to remind you—from time to time—to check if you're having the impact you intended.

— VIKI MERRICK, CO-PRODUCER OF *THE MOTH RADIO HOUR*

Elisabeth Swan's new book, *Picture Yourself a Leader*, is full of charm, wit, intelligence, and guidance for achieving real leadership qualities. Elisabeth is a true mentor, and her book provides insights into ways to manage change more effectively, discover how to better guide problem solvers, and how to become a valued leader. Using a thought-provoking collection of mini-stories, the book illustrates leadership principles and provides a roadmap to achieving your personal leadership goals. A must-read for anyone interested in being a change agent in our ever-changing world.

— MIRIAM WEISMAN, PROFESSOR OF BUSINESS LAW AND TAX AT FLORIDA INTERNATIONAL UNIVERSITY

As leaders, it is hard to anticipate all the stumbles you'll make, especially when leading people through change. In *Picture Yourself a Leader*, Elisabeth captures relatable lessons through storytelling. The flexible format allows readers to digest the content that aligns best with their needs. Need a warm-up activity for a team meeting? Development on a specific topic? Curious what other experts think? You get it all right here! A must-have for anyone in leadership or aspiring to grow to that next level.

— SALLY TOISTER, RETIRED HOSPITALITY
OPERATIONS EXECUTIVE

PICTURE YOURSELF A LEADER

Illustrated Micro-Lessons for Navigating Change

ELISABETH SWAN

LUMEN PRESS

Picture Yourself a Leader: Illustrated Micro-Lessons for Navigating Change

Written and Illustrated by Elisabeth Swan
Cover by Madelyn Copperwaite, MC Creative LLC
Typesetting by Stephanie Feger, emPower PR Group
Copy Editing by Brian Manning

First Edition, April 2023
ISBN: 979-8-9876627-0-0
Library of Congress Control Number: 2023906026
Created in the United States of America

Learn more about Elisabeth Swan and how she can support you in your own change efforts by visiting www.elisabethswan.com. Special discounts are available on quantity book purchases. Contact Elisabeth@elisabethswan.com.

DEDICATION

To my husband Scott, my moral superior and fearless partner who's game for it all. I got lucky.

To my late friend Bennett Neimen who taught me that I could do anything.

And to my undaunted mother, my hero and a model for how to grab life and shake it until you get a prize.

CONTENTS

PICTURE THIS

When Tracy O'Rourke and I wrote *The Problem-Solver's Toolkit*, we outlined the basic tools that problem solvers needed to fix a process. What we learned from readers was that some of the most useful tidbits they got from the book were based on what we dubbed *potholes*. Traps people might fall into during their journey, along with the *detours* that could get them back on track. Consider this your personal *pothole-detour* primer.

The true challenges exist in the humanity underlying our efforts. We're not simply practitioners. We're flawed human beings trying to be our best selves and make good choices. We may follow the right steps and still see our efforts fall short. That's where leadership makes the difference.

And the word "leader" can mean many things. It's not necessarily associated with a slot on an organizational chart. Leading a life makes you a leader. There are influential problem solvers who may not consider themselves leaders—yet they are. And there are leaders who don't see that problem solving is what they do all day long.

ORIGINS OF THE BOOK

Picture Yourself a Leader was born of lessons learned over a lifetime. It captures the potholes and resulting detours I've experienced at home, working with others, consulting, coaching, or simply living in the world. This collection of stories is my ever-present guide, and it's time to share it.

During the thick of the COVID-19 pandemic, like many others, I had to deal with unexpected career changes. I turned to writing and drawing as an outlet for exploring what I brought to the table. Each week I shaped a reflection and shared a lesson learned along with my own illustration of the pain, paradox, or humanity behind the issue— and maybe a little humor. I posted them on LinkedIn and ended each post with a question for the broader community. The goal was to learn how others approached that week's issue.

Each topic led to unexpected conversations, new insights, and alternative takes on the challenge. Many suggested gathering my posts and illustrations into a book. I wanted that book too, and I wanted to include the nuggets that sprang up during the exchanges. This book is richer as a result of the kindness, gameness, and wisdom of the contributors.

PERSONAL PROBLEM SOLVING

My professional community consists of people dedicated to problem solving. This includes recognizable industry names; Continuous Improvement, Operational Excellence, Toyota Kata, Lean, and Six Sigma. I've included a glossary in case these sound foreign. Regardless of the title, when practiced well, the approaches are grounded in systematic observation, measurement, and experimentation to solve complex issues or achieve objectives when the solution is unknown. Whether you approach it with structure or not—and regardless of the label—problem solving is something every human being engages in on some level every day.

The approaches are sound, although the potholes remain. What matters is things like how we treat people, what we say to them, how they interpret the words we use, what we choose to focus on, and how we do it. The improvement models are great guides but we're often missing instructions for surmounting personal roadblocks. For those hurdles it helps to examine our often unconscious ways of operating. Are these intangibles serving us well? Or should we consider new ways of making things happen.

A METHOD TO THE MADNESS

Why did I illustrate each chapter? Aside from the fun of it, our brains process images tens of thousands times faster than text. They stimulate our imagination, make abstract ideas tangible, and change our mood and perception of a message. That's why we click on videos, post photos, and visit museums more than libraries. Images engage us.

Each illustration is paired with a story. Stories are what bind us together. If I tell you about the time I struggled to hold my tongue, you may not have been there, but you know how it felt. Storytelling is participatory, immersive, and if the story is good, entertaining. There's no need for education to be a slog.

The combination of images and stories anchors each topic. The chapters offer insights and prompts so you can consider your own story and how you might adapt it. Experimentation is an inescapable part of problem solving. Trial and error are equally practical when trying out new habits. You get to toss what's outlived its usefulness and keep what you like.

This started out as weekly posts to keep my own learning alive, and they still exist in that format. The conversation continues. The goal is that by reading these stories, and challenging your own thinking, you'll be able to move toward a mindset that will bring you greater peace of mind, better performance, a bigger support community, and hopefully some of the success and joy you seek.

WHO SHOULD USE THIS?

Picture Yourself a Leader is intended to be a resource for people at all stages of life. We're all leaders—of something. It may be within our families, in our friendship circles, or in ways we're unaware of. You don't need a title, or have people reporting to you, to be a person with influence. This book helps the leadership journeys of aspiring leaders, managers of problem solvers, organizational leaders, and those who don't realize they're already leaders. It's designed to spark thought and conversation at all levels.

Do you need to be conversant in the language of structured problem solving? No.

Having read through and discussed these topics with others it's clear that the dialogue crosses industries, fields, roles, and walks of life.

I've discussed mindset with representatives of human resources, traded innovation techniques with engineers, gotten great tips on communication from customer service experts, and received productivity techniques from people in marketing, and the "potholes" we hit are universal. Most people face the challenges addressed throughout these pages regardless of their titles, day jobs, or lack thereof.

This book is for anyone who wants to work and play more effectively with others. If you do, you are bound to find insights throughout to inspire you to create a better picture of yourself ... as a leader.

CHOOSE YOUR OWN ADVENTURE

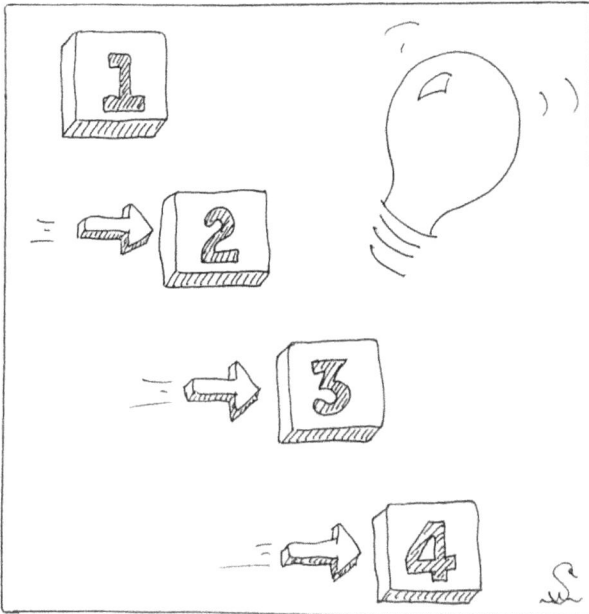

There are at least half-a-dozen ways you can use this book. This chapter throws out a few suggestions, and you get to approach it in the way that best serves you. We are all unique ... in how we see the world, in how we see ourselves, and in how we see our work. Our singularity makes the world tick. With that truth in mind, make this book align with your individual needs. Welcome to a leader's *choose your own adventure* journey.

THE BASIC JOURNEY

Take in the Illustration and Story

The image may strike a chord, and the story might remind you of a similar moment in your own life. Together, these elements will ground you in a potentially familiar pothole followed by a bit of resulting wisdom. Each story ends with a question posed to the community.

Embrace the Wisdom of the Crowd

Colleagues from around the world engaged in an open forum on each topic. The contributors ranged from front-line problem solvers to authors and thought leaders. The curated responses provide additional resources, techniques, suggested books, and different ways to consider the challenge at hand. It's an extra layer of insights to draw on.

Capture Your Ideas

Following each story, there's an "Ink Makes You Think" section. In this case the "ink" is a combination of elements; the ink of the illustration, the ink of the story, and the ink of your own notes. Research shows that the act of physically writing things down helps you take in what you're reading. It results in more robust brain activity. It also impacts your ability to retain information and recall what you've read. There's also the extra consideration in putting pen to paper since there's intent in deciding which words to use. Gotta think.

Experiment

These insights and resources are here for you to try a new way of operating. Take action on a personal shift you'd like to make. It could be a tweak to what you currently do. Try it on your own. Bring it to the team. Test it during a morning huddle. Little steps and experiments lead to bigger changes. Consider what you want to see happen, and then reflect on how it worked out.

INDIVIDUAL GROWTH OPTIONS

The Weekly Reader

Whereas the posts were initially spontaneous, the topics have been organized to follow a natural progression. You can start from the very beginning and address the challenges in order. Fifty micro-lessons means you get to create a weekly schedule. There's exactly enough for one year, with time off for a well-deserved vacation.

The Cherry Picker

Use the book to navigate a specific issue. There are a range of categories to choose from. Is a co-worker driving you batty? You might want to skip to Chapter 12—Get Curious About Conflict. Are you tired of not getting credit for doing a great job? Try out Chapter 49—Participate! Culture is a Contact Sport.

- Scan the Table of Contents for titles that spark interest.
- Look up keywords like "Conflict" or "Credit," in the Index.
- Go directly to the Chapter, or Chapters, to address a pressing issue.

You can tackle typical problem-solving snags, consider your approach to productivity, recharge your creative process, contemplate the impact of your mindset on others, or spend time reflecting on how you relate to yourself.

WORKING WITH GROUPS

The Teacher Feature

Use these stories in workshops and classes. Each Chapter serves to make a point. As a tribe, we humans are storytellers. Colleagues, students, and participants benefit from models and systems. Stories bring those elements to life. Feel free to use these stories to illuminate and illustrate.

As an example, if participants are struggling with the fear of making mistakes, try introducing Chapter 42—Morph Gaffes into Gems. If people are stuck on some screw up, you could check out Chapter 37—Go from Setback to Insight. Telling stories helps share vulnerabilities and makes room for laughter. Make them work for you as you work with other humans.

The Jump Starter

Use the questions as warm-up activities. When working with groups it's important to start sessions in alignment. Whether it's onsite or online, people arrive to meetings and workshops with their minds and energy in disparate places. The stories and questions help to set the tone. You can use just the right chapter to bring them together with a common purpose.

1. Select a Topic

Scan either the Table of Contents or the Index for relevant topics. Choose a chapter that relates to the task at hand. As an example, if the group is struggling with listening skills, you might select Chapter 11—Beware the Illusion of Listening.

2. Read the Story

Read the story, or your own variation, to the group.

3. Assign the Question

Ask them the question posed in the "Wisdom of the Crowd" section for that Chapter, such as, "What are some methods you use to make people feel appreciated?" Depending upon the group size, you can either conduct the discussion with the larger group or put them into remote or onsite breakout groups to discuss their responses.

4. Debrief the Reactions & Next Steps

Ask the participants what personal change they plan to make based on their discussion of the topic. You can ask a question posed in "Ink Makes You Think" such as, "Consider someone you haven't recognized lately. What might you say to them?" Encourage them to start small—a simple shift.

The Huddle Anchor

If you conduct daily huddles (quick group meetings, generally held while standing), you can use the chapters as regular thought-provokers. Select the top five areas of need, and address one topic a day for a week.

1. Select a Topic

Scan either the Table of Contents or the Index for relevant topics. Choose a chapter that relates to the recurring themes. As an example, if people are feeling underappreciated, you might select Chapter 34 —Be Generous in Your Praise.

2. Read the Story

You can read the story to the group and, if possible, display the image.

3. Ask the Question

Ask them the same question posed to the "Crowd" for that Chapter and discuss as a group: "What are some methods you use to make people feel appreciated?" Help your colleagues, the team, department, or managerial group get in the habit of questioning the way they operate. This could be a discussion, or you could ask them to draw images of their reactions.

4. Try Something and See What You Learn

Based on what the group decides to experiment with, you could add a new step to regular meetings, video calls, the Huddle Board, or wherever appropriate. In this example, the group might opt to recognize a team member at the start of each meetup.

THE ILLUSTRATIONS

The illustrations are mine, and hopefully they inspire you to draw! But if not, and you'd like to use them, I'd be honored. If you do, please include an attribution, "Illustration by Elisabeth Swan" is fine. Of course, please don't use them for commercial purposes, put them on websites, or post them on social media. If you have any questions about using them, just reach out to me.

LET ME KNOW HOW IT GOES

Experiment. Make each micro-lesson work for you. If you come up with a new way to use the lessons, let me know about it, and let me know about your results. How did you apply it? What did you learn? What were the benefits?

Reach out to me at www.ElisabethSwan.com.

Are you ready? Let's do this!

Part One

CONSIDER YOUR ACTIONS

As you work with others, it helps to know where they're struggling, and that's not always apparent. On the flip side, what might appear obvious to you may seem foreign to your colleagues. You may describe a path to success, but they may not hear it the way you intended. It helps to meet people where they are, though you might not be sure exactly where that is. Addressing common challenges can be a start. You can learn and be of assistance as you talk through their pain points. These stories and accompanying questions offer potential pathways.

As usual, there are options and an ever-evolving *current best way*. You'll benefit from hearing how others navigate change and gain from their insights.

1. Let the Structure Set You Free
Structure, paradoxically, enables freedom.

2. Listen, Customers Are Talking
Do you truly understand what they want?

3. Clarify the Problem
"Lack of" is a solution masquerading as a problem.

4. Beware the Lure of the Quick Fix
Help those around you to pause and reflect.

5. Share the Underlying Purpose
People need to understand the "why" behind their efforts.

6. Do It Right—Don't Do It Over
Are people getting good at things they shouldn't be doing at all?

7. Dig the Best Path to Root Causes
Focus where it makes sense, not where it's easy.

8. Question the Process Before Automating It
Are we speeding up a bad thing?

9. Stay Open to New Best Ways
How do people determine standards?

10. Use Surveys Wisely
Likert scales lack essential detail.

1

LET THE STRUCTURE SET YOU FREE

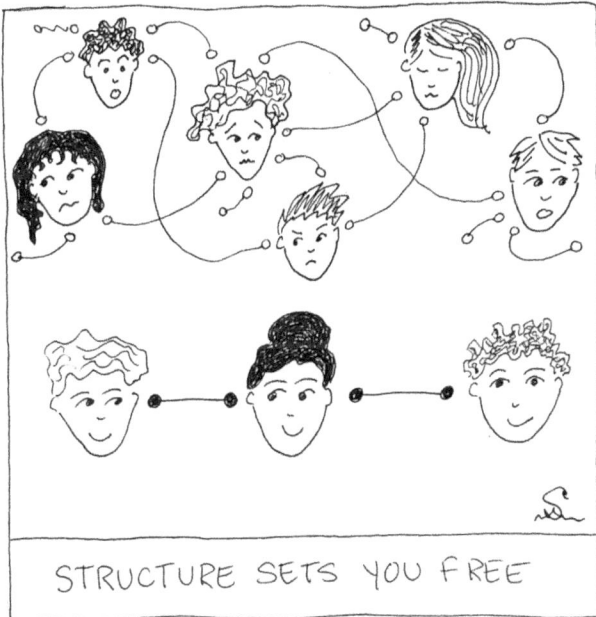

STRUCTURE SETS YOU FREE

"STRUCTURE SETS YOU FREE" IS AN ADAGE FROM MY EARLY DAYS ON STAGE AS PART OF AN IMPROV TROUPE.

Ending up with ImprovBoston for many years is a story in itself. Witnessing the troupe for the first time was a mind-blowing experience. How did they know what to say? It was a scriptless riot. Whole scenes out of nothing—an effortless comedic tour-de-force.

That hooked me good. After joining one of their workshops, the troupe soon had me performing with the cast. The experience exposed the effort required.

The truth is that improv does *not* emerge from thin air, it's built upon rules, structure, and constraints.

It's one of those seeming paradoxes: restriction frees the imagination. ImprovBoston introduced me to a host of rules: "say yes—and," "forward the plot," "listen," and so on. They guided each improvised scene with a different structure. Structures had names like "Translator," "Foreign Film Dub" and "Hitchhiker" and they provided rules and roles. As an example, Translator had two roles: One person from a made-up country who spoke gibberish about a given topic, and a second person who translated what they said for the audience. Never got tired of that one.

If we didn't follow a given structure, walked into an imaginary prop, or broke the rules, we got notes at the end of the night. It was experimentation in its purest form, and the structure helped us perfect our craft.

Having a structure doesn't bind you—the reverse is true. It frees you up to plan, invent, experiment, and push against boundaries. At the peak of my improv career, we were performing completely improvised musicals with protagonists, events, obstacles, transformations, and resolutions—and a mess of songs we made up on the spot. None of that spontaneous invention was remotely possible without constant practice and structure.

The rules of improv apply generously to life. You should be moving the plot forward, you must listen to and be respectful to those around you, and it's not a good idea to stand there being a talking head. The rules of improv remain instruments for the stage, but their existence bolsters the idea that structure is essential to making things happen. Once you have structure you can cut loose.

In contrast, when problem solvers *wing it*, they generally jump to a solution without truly understanding what they're solving. It's analogous to skipping the scenes, any character development, and proceeding directly to the resolution. There's a chance they'll succeed —maybe the solution "scene" was so great it could stand on its own with no plot. But more likely they create rework, confusion, and waste people's time.

Problem solvers benefit from structures like PDCA (Plan Do Check Adjust), DMAIC (Define, Measure, Analyze, Improve, Control), Agile, or any host of 3-, 4-, 5-, and 6-step methods. Even if they don't follow them lockstep, structures provide a framework to push up against.

To get along in the world, you've got calendars, to-do lists, and alarm clocks—or is that simply your phone? Apps tell you what's due, when to leave the house or simply what day it is. You need structure— without boundaries you risk the immobilization of a blank page. The same goes for those you work with. Part of the journey is to push against limits.

Structure is good for mental health, because not having boundaries is like pushing on a rope.

———

THE WISDOM OF THE CROWD

How do you use structure to set others free?

I definitely push for structure which sometimes makes me feel guilty but no more after reading this! My favorite and most effective way to apply structure is the recurring meeting! A fantastically simple way to keep momentum.

—Emmie Fox, Senior Business Process Analyst, Zurich North America

I create structure by building standards in the organization. They are the foundation to good communication and measurement in your organization. I like to use a workflow app for planning purposes and team collaboration, then Kata and PDCA for solving operational and process problems. Without structure, you have to constantly react, so the blame game becomes the norm.

—Eric Ducroix, Lean Six Sigma Expert

I've inherited issues that were 'solved' once, twice, or three times. They failed to implement standards to keep those improvements in place so things fell back to where they used to be or got worse. I've heard people say, 'we had a Kaizen (Rapid Improvement Event) and trained people two years ago.' Yes, but the people from two years ago are no longer in the same role, and we didn't create systematic training to ensure that *new* people got trained on the process. This makes me double down on structure. You have to see it through to the Control Phase—structure sets you free if you follow it.

—Pilar Zimmerman, Operational Excellence Senior Manager at Illumina

REFLECTIONS

You can debate the merit of the different structures to work within, but those standardized methods remain linchpins of productive work. You may boomerang between rigidity and chaos, but even if you feel you are at your most imaginative when improvising, you've most likely got practice and experience to base it on. When people are new to a pursuit, they rely on others to provide boundaries. They are looking to you for the guideposts to stray from.

INK MAKES YOU THINK

- Where do you see the need for structure?
- What is one type of structure you could experiment with this week to help guide the path for yourself, or those looking to you for guidance?
- What will you see if the experiment works?

2

LISTEN, CUSTOMERS ARE TALKING

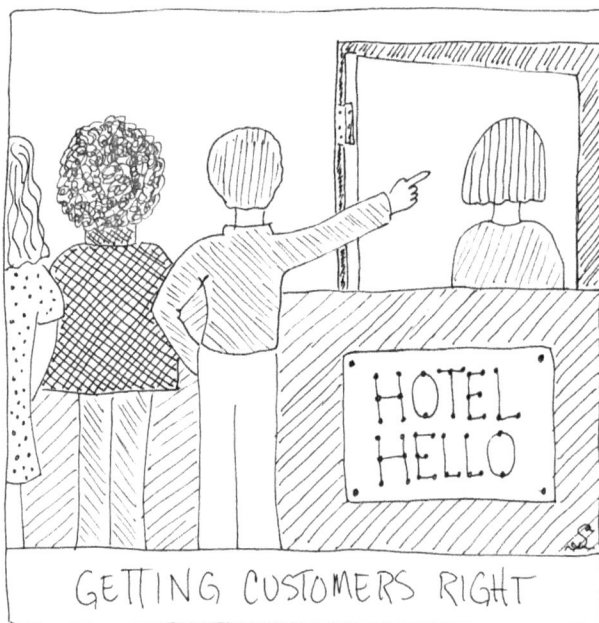

GETTING CUSTOMERS RIGHT

DO YOU TRULY KNOW WHAT CUSTOMERS WANT?

I remember getting it wrong while working as part of a large team of process-improvement consultants. We conducted a proof-of-concept project for a multinational hotel chain. It was in support of their continuous improvement rollout, and the "starter project" was reducing guest check-in time at one of their properties. It was exciting to be involved with the transformation kickoff, and it felt familiar. As consultants-for-hire, we'd become "road warriors"— hotels were our second homes.

Considering what has to happen, hotel check-in should take about two minutes, which seemed like a reasonable target. The clock started when a person got in line, and it ended when they got their room key. That felt logical. The project took life.

Knowing the voice of the customer was key, which meant interviewing guests after they'd checked in. The questions revolved around how long they had waited to get their key, and how they felt about the experience. The conversations led somewhere else.

The guests told a different story. They didn't mind waiting in line as long as everyone at the front desk appeared to be helping someone— the two-minute target didn't seem to matter that much. They got irritated when desk agents failed to make eye contact (imagine that scene in the movie, *Meet the Fockers* when Ben Stiller is anxiously waiting at the airport gate while the gate agent types endlessly— never looking up). And they were annoyed by agents disappearing through *that door* behind the front desk—they got frustrated having to wait if agents kept stepping in and out—and where were they going anyway?!

Their reactions were unexpected and revealed our assumptions. It seemed like a simple cycle-time reduction effort, but time was not the main thing on people's minds. It left me with a lasting sense of humility and steady sense of curiosity whenever approaching an improvement opportunity.

When you are working with others, you may find a familiar attitude about the customers of any given process. People often feel confident about what the customer wants. The problem is that if they're wrong —even a little—it can misdirect the entire effort, or miss out on truly helping customers.

Things are not always what they seem.

_____

THE WISDOM OF THE CROWD

What is an example of a time when a group got it wrong with their customers?

> As you point out, a customer's experience with wait time is both the actual time spent waiting and their perception of the wait. Faster is usually better, but we can also alter the perception. What this points out is that wait time is not the only thing people care about. They want to be acknowledged. They want to see that people are making an effort.
>
> —Jeff Toister, Author of *The Service Culture Handbook*

> I worked at a manufacturing company where there were different Service Level Agreements (SLAs) set up with each large customer. It created a lot of confusion in production, and we moved mountains to avoid fees by trying to achieve tight timelines. When our sales team returned to the customers and asked if they would accept our standard SLAs. They shrugged and said, 'sure.' Since we didn't offer SLAs from the start, they simply picked metrics out of thin air. As I incorporate this learning into a transactional environment, I've

discovered this variable SLA sales practice is extremely common.

—Stephanie Hill, Owner of Lightbulb Moment Consulting

We pursued customer excellence in one company, and we made significant improvements in 'the time taken for delivery.' We took it from three weeks to two weeks, to one week, and finally down to three days. Surprisingly, when we sought the customers' feedback, we found customers didn't mind waiting for three days or one week for this particular type of business. What they truly wanted was to be given a specific date and time for delivery, so they weren't left waiting for the delivery man to show up!

—Khalil Al Fardan, Visionary Leader and Business Solutions Provider at Etisalat

REFLECTIONS

It's easy to get it *wrong* when making assumptions about customer needs. You need to encourage people to go to the source—and talk to customers. Spend time thinking through all aspects of a customer's experience. Issues like wait time are not all people care about. People want to be acknowledged. They want to feel seen. They want to see others making an effort. It's important for people to consider what "acknowledgement" looks like in a given process, and how to meet that requirement. The way to discovery starts with the person receiving the goods and services. It's important to guide people back to that source.

INK MAKES YOU THINK

- Have you, or those you work with, checked in with the customer lately?
- What questions would test assumptions about what the customer truly wants?
- What do you expect to hear?

3

CLARIFY THE PROBLEM

IS "LACK OF TRAINING" THE ISSUE?

Lack of anything is a solution masquerading as a problem. There's always *some* training required once you've come up with a better way to do something, yet lack of training is almost never the core issue or the solution.

It reminds me of an instructor at my local gym. She was a young, fit, fabulous workout leader, and she had a nagging issue with the lot of us. She was tired of fishing our plastic water bottles from the trash (fear not—most of us brought reusable water bottles).

"This is not the recycling bin people!" She spent time at the end of each workout explaining. "Trash is on the *left*, and recycling is on the *right*! Got it? Trash left. Recycle right." She repeated the instructions with a slightly exasperated smile.

She saw the problem as a training issue. She repeated the instructions regularly, hoping that someday we'd finally get it. Are you wondering if the bins were different colors? No, they weren't. Did they have icons or labels for trash and recycling? Nope and nope. So clearly there was a knowledge gap. We didn't know which bins to use for what. And sadly, our "bin-training" sessions were not having the desired impact. It was hard enough getting the spin-class sessions to have the desired impact.

This same assumption emerges with problem solvers. They see "lack of training" as a problem or a root cause. By doing that, they've narrowed their options in terms of uncovering the true issue. They've also limited themselves in terms of how they might solve the problem.

Framing the problem as lack of training limits the solution to … training. What if they framed the issue as a *knowledge gap?* Clarifying the true problem alters their perspective for the better. A knowledge gap could be filled with things other than training; a sign, a series of visuals, color indicators, automated cues.

A helpful way to frame the issue is to remind people that the best form of training is—no training. Seek ways to make the process obvious and intuitive so that people automatically know what to do.

Did anyone teach you how to use a drive-thru? Did you need instructions on how to order something from Amazon? Make the process self-explanatory and you'll minimize the need to train.

––––––

THE WISDOM OF THE CROWD

How do you help people move beyond the "lack of training is the problem" mentality?

> Anytime people jump to RE-training as a solution, I have to ask, "If it didn't work the first time, why would doing it again be different?"

—Jamie Flinchbaugh, Author of *People Solve Problems*

> There are four reasons people don't do what's wanted, in order.
>
> 1. Don't know *what* is wanted.
>
> 2. Don't know *how* to do what is wanted.
>
> 3. Don't have the *ability* to do what is wanted.
>
> 4. Don't *want* to do what is wanted.
>
> Most leaders presume the issue is either Option 4 or lack of training which is Option 2. But most of the time the issue is Option 1. As a result, my opening question is almost always, "How do you know that they actually know what you want them to do?"

—Hugh Alley, Author of *Becoming the Supervisor*

Through the years, we've identified what we call 'usual suspect solutions'—comfortable but often misguided actions that people assume will make things better, but sadly, often fail. Training—along with reorganization—is at the top of the list. Repeated training on a bad or confusing process is a waste of time. Much better to look for better ways to do things. Or—when the process is what it is—focus on extending the learning and reinforcement to help people apply the learning.

—Pete Pande, Author of *The Six Sigma Way* and President of Pivotal Resources, Inc.

REFLECTIONS

The trick is to have questions and techniques to push past "lack of training" as a problem or a place to start. Some simply ban the phrases *"lack of"* or *"need more,"* along with a long list of ready-made solutions. What helps is to reframe the issue as an "issue" as opposed to the "lack of" [fill in the solution]. That encourages people to see more possibilities, and reach for higher levels of creativity.

INK MAKES YOU THINK

- Prepare yourself for "lack of training" posed as a problem.
- What is one question you could ask people you work with to redirect their creativity?
- What would spark their interest?
- How would you know it worked?

4

BEWARE THE LURE OF THE QUICK FIX

DON'T BRING ME A PROBLEM, BRING ME A SOLUTION

"DON'T BRING ME A PROBLEM, BRING ME A SOLUTION."

It sounds like a good idea, but is it?

The most common example I run into is people moving from problem to solution so quickly that it's hard to decipher the problem. "The problem is lack of automation" is becoming an increasingly familiar refrain. Automation can be a huge game changer, but without clarifying which problem it's solving, it might create new issues. One recent technology fix resulted in the need for triple entry of the same data into three different systems. Yet there remains a steady stream of folks primed to jump immediately to the solution. And it's fun!

Coming up with ideas is exciting. The problem is that going directly from problem to solution is like the marathon runner who took a bus to the finish line.

It means missing the entire race. The odds of getting the fix right without any due diligence are low. The likelihood of having to rework your efforts is high. Yet many people had managers who encouraged them to do just that. Don't bring me a problem, bring me a solution. There's an army of employees trained to leap immediately to the finish line.

Without having any experience with structured problem solving, people often present solutions in the guise of problem statements. They're not aware of what goes into studying processes, talking to stakeholders, or digging to the root cause. If those things are foreign you might hear problems phrased like this:

- "The problem is we need a monitoring system for the intake process."
- "The problem is that we need to retrain the staff on the process."
- "The problem is we need an inspection step."

This is how a lot of folks are trained to address problems—with an immediate solution. It can take a bit of digging to uncover the true issue. One way to uncover problems is to ask exactly what they're solving:

- What would a monitoring system solve?
- What would retraining the staff address?
- What would an inspection step allow us to fix?

The answers might be:

- We aren't responding to customers on time.
- Staff don't know where to find supplies.
- We're making mistakes on the intake form.

Now *those* sound like problems. And maybe the monitoring systems, the training, and the inspection would help, but how would you know if you don't know *why* those things are happening? Being able to clarify the problem takes practice and some guidance. The beauty of problem-solving models is that they provide a structure to investigate process issues. PDCA: Plan, Do, Check, Act or DMAIC: Define, Measure, Analyze, Improve, and Control are two common structures.

Solutions for both of these models come *after* you've studied the process. The Plan phase of PDCA includes digging to the root cause before coming up with countermeasures in the Do phase. DMAIC includes the Analyze phase before solving the problem during the Improve phase. If you truly know the solution, you could simply put it in place and be done with it. No need for problem solving if the problem is solved, right?

Helping people get clarity around a problem requires them to unlearn their jump-to-solution education. They have to unlearn one habit—that's been rewarded in the past—and learn a new one that is foreign and seems tougher. It's not one-and-done. It takes patience and repetition.

Solving things feels rewarding. Maybe a person has the best idea right out of the gate without doing *any* analysis or talking to *any* process participants. But how many times have you seen knee-jerk solutions implemented that didn't resolve the issue? It's a waste of people's time, it's often a waste of cash, and sometimes it makes things worse. It definitely saps the spirits of those involved.

Solving problems is our job as human beings. For some of us it's our profession. So why do we stumble here? It's exciting to leap into action. The glory is in improving. There's boldness and bravery in change. When it works, you're helping people.

The people you work with often unwittingly skip looking at *why* the issue is truly happening when they have a cool idea. Offering solutions instead of problems sounds reasonable. You know intellectually it doesn't work that way, but it feels mean to muffle the spirits of people who are offering answers before studying the problem. The disappointment is palpable. "We're not there yet." is a deflating rallying cry. The efficiency of an instant answer is a mirage, so it's your job to keep yourself and others honest.

THE WISDOM OF THE CROWD

How do you help problem solvers resist the glory of *the quick fix* to focus on root causes?

> When you're an expert root cause problem solver there is very little fame and fanfare. Others rarely know that you prevented something big from happening. So, to encourage this behavior, organizations need to become more creative at celebrating these hidden successes. One immediate impact of preventing problems vs. reacting to them is in the reduced level of stress and the increased control we have over our day. We must shift

our mindset. We need to feel proud about controlling our day vs. saving the day.

—Jennifer Ayers, Executive Director of the Northwest High Performance Enterprise Consortium (NWHPEC)

From my experience there are two questions that hold the power to make people in a firefighting culture pause; 'Is this really the question we should be trying to answer? Is this really the problem we should be trying to solve?' Asking these helps to raise awareness of the importance of identifying the problem *first* before jumping to solutions.

—Sabrina Malter, Business Coach & Consultant at Unveil Business Consulting GmbH

I remind people that it's 'fake glory' if the solution doesn't work. So, how about we make sure it really works and it solves the root cause!

—Tracy O'Rourke, Co-Author of *The Problem-Solver's Toolkit*

REFLECTIONS

One way to counteract a culture that encourages jumping to a solution is to teach people how to properly clarify the problem. "A Problem Well Stated is Half Solved" per Charles Kettering of General Motors. Another idea is to reward reflection and problem solving. That means honoring people who use their inquiry skills. Another technique, that's less visible, is to count the number of questions asked during meetings. There are organizations who host monthly meetings to showcase problem solvers describing their successful journeys. It takes time and intention but there's more of that to go around when there are not as many fires to put out.

INK MAKES YOU THINK

- What question could you ask about a quick fix to understand the thinking behind it?
- What is one way to reward those you work with for resisting the easy fix?
- What's something you could say or do this week to encourage at least one person to spend time understanding what's in the way?

5

SHARE THE UNDERLYING PURPOSE

DO THEY KNOW WHY? DO PEOPLE UNDERSTAND THE REASONS YOU WANT TO CHANGE THINGS?

Simon Sinek built a career around starting with "why." People are more interested in *why* you are doing something, than *what* you're doing or *how*. We know it matters, but we often fail to clarify it to others, or even ourselves.

I was coaching an office manager at a childcare nonprofit, and she was growing increasingly dispirited by resistance to her efforts to reduce expenses. She described the purchasing process as, "Buy As You Wish." People had access to the company credit card so they could buy supplies when they needed them. It helped everyone manage essential services, but as she toured the facilities she saw the downsides.

There were daycare centers with dishwashers while they still ordered paper plates and plastic utensils. Staff ordered from a broad mix of vendors, which limited her efforts to get bulk discounts. The Office Manager saw savings opportunities, so she experimented. She purchased a new cleanser for all the facilities, and was blindsided by the backlash.

"I don't like the smell."
"It irritates my skin."
"Why are you doing this?"

As Office Manager she had zero positional authority, so she asked the CEO for support and got it. But the process felt like gearing up for battle. She dreaded the prospect of requiring teachers to go through her to get the staples they needed. Her shoulders sagged at the prospect.

Then she did some math that changed her tune. The next time we spoke there was a smile on her face. She had calculated how much money it would take to afford a mortgage for a new daycare center. It was one of the year's biggest goals and it was within reach. A new facility would mean helping more kids. She was excited—this was good news for everyone.

She shared her thoughts at the next staff meeting. The mood shifted and she felt less like a combatant. This gave her the courage to revisit the "cleanser issue." She offered up a new product she'd researched and passed it around the table. She let them know this particular soap was being used in Neonatal Intensive Care Units (NICU), and they agreed it was worth testing out.

She told me that after that meeting, colleagues began approaching her with money-saving ideas—now she had inspired collaborators. They not only hit their goal within the month, they got the mortgage for the new facility, and they were able to give staff long-overdue raises.

It reinforced how critical it is for people to clarify why stakeholders should care about their improvement efforts. Barriers to change are real, but some are self-inflicted.

It helps to consider why it's worth doing something. "For the sake of what?" It might require peeling back a few layers to get to a fitting purpose, but it challenges problem solvers to imagine the impact of their efforts and get to a compelling "*why*."

––––––

THE WISDOM OF THE CROWD

How do you encourage others to clarify the "why" of a change effort?

> It's not just 'the why'... people need to cooperate towards a common goal. They need to feel, and know, they are contributing to something bigger, like purchasing a new childcare center. As we say in *Toyota Way to Service Excellence*, you can't reduce your way into

service excellence. No one is excited about having something taken away. No one will care about reducing expenses for the sake of reducing expenses. I worked for one company that called it 'expense excellence,' to no avail. People want to contribute! When they get together and use their creativity for the positive, the possibilities are endless!

—Karyn Ross, Activator and Author of *The Kind Leader*

The lessons in this story align with something I encourage leaders and coaches to do—be explicit about what they are doing and the "why" behind it. This can take many forms, from being clear on the direction the organization needs to go and why it's important, or the reason behind a management decision. Or this could be by 'labeling'—describing why they are acting in a certain way—such as asking questions or pausing. Especially if it is different from how they might have acted in the past. If we don't make the invisible thinking behind our actions visible to others, then it can lead to assumptions of our intention.

—Katie Anderson, Leadership Consultant and Author of *Learning to Lead, Leading to Learn*

I once worked with a production team tasked with reducing their spend on overtime. The operators assumed this was a simple money-saving exercise instigated by management. Management assumed the operators just wanted the extra cash from the overtime. When we got everyone in a room and discussed the wants and needs of both sides, we discovered that neither had assumed correctly. We had great discussions and clarified a 'why' based on having a smooth day and getting all staff home safely, on time, with smiles on their faces.

—Gemma Jones, Improvement Coach and Founder of SPARK Improvement Ltd.

REFLECTIONS

Understanding the *why*, and how change benefits not only the individual but the community and the people they care about, is key. It takes some effort to get that clarity. Those we are leading often assume the benefit is obvious, so we need to help them see that it's worth spelling it out. Asking leading questions like "and I should care because ..." can help them raise their perspective to a level that matters to others. It's a process, but if they take the time, people pay attention.

INK MAKES YOU THINK

- Think of a project you've been involved in. Does everyone understand why they're doing it?
- Are people aware of their intentions?
- How could you tell if everyone understands the "*why*?"

6

DO IT RIGHT—DON'T DO IT OVER

ARE PEOPLE PERFECTING REWORK?

Do people unwittingly plan to get things wrong and then perfect "the fix?" Do they sometimes pride themselves on getting good at constantly correcting the things they're doing wrong? What if instead of getting good at rework, they took the time to prevent the problem from happening in the first place? The words of Jack Bergman ring true, "There's never enough time to do it right, but there's always enough time to do it over."

I remember being impressed with one of the most well-thought-out rework loops I'd ever seen during a night out. My husband and I got caught in Boston traffic on our way to see a friend's son in a play. He was the lead in a play at Harvard University's ART (American Repertory Theater), and we were stressed we'd miss the start and not be allowed into the theater. After a few lucky left turns, some inspired parking—and a sprint—we breezed in just in time.

The friendly woman at the ticket counter immediately handed us a xeroxed sheet of paper with a street map. There was a yellow-highlighted path through Harvard Square. She explained that the play was at a separate ART theater, and staff would help us once we got there. We had come to the wrong theater, but she was ready for us.

Frustrated and convinced we had officially missed the opening scene, we hoofed it through winding sidewalks, dodged pedestrians, and rushed into the new lobby as my hair gave up any pretense of glamor. Greeted once again by a calm, friendly woman, we noticed a group of eight other winded people all holding the same xeroxed map in their hands.

The kind staffer directed us to wait five more minutes until there was a *lights-out* moment in the play. At that point, she would lead us all by penlight to the front row where they'd reserved seats for those of us who'd gone to the wrong theater.

We got to see the play—and admire the young breakout star—from the best seats in the house. I was thrilled, and the play was a revelation. What stuck with me was their impressive process for fixing the seemingly common mistake of patrons going to the wrong theater. They had this *rework loop* down. But did they need to? Why were so many of us running frantically through the square?

Given my background (and hair situation), it felt appropriate to consider the root cause of our misadventure. The main graphic on the printed tickets was a big, bold "ART" which was the theater we first ran into. The theater we were *supposed* to go to was listed in small print much lower in the email. That simple visual miscue may have so consistently led patrons astray that they crafted an elegant course correction complete with highlighted street maps. With a built-in bonus of front-row seats!

What if instead, the email had immediately highlighted the *right* theater? What if the visuals pointed out the address that ticket holders should head to? We might have been in our original seats, on time, with a better parking spot. The seats wouldn't have been as good, but my hair might have survived.

How often do our colleagues hone rework loops instead of considering what's causing the mistake? When are they setting themselves up to make the diving catch instead of removing the need for the dive? Customers often love people for saving the day. People plan for fire—but are they the unwitting arsonists?

Yes, every system could benefit from a contingency plan, but that's not the first place to focus.

———

THE WISDOM OF THE CROWD

Where have you seen people getting comfortable with rework?

I was working with a department to identify the key processes in their area, so we knew where to focus improvement efforts. The team insisted that their #1 key process was rework. If they couldn't get the parts reworked and back to their downstream customer within an hour, the downstream lines could shut down. They prided themselves on how well they could do the rework process to ensure their downstream customer was satisfied. They wanted to get even faster at rework instead of focusing on elimination of rework entirely. As you can imagine, this led to some great discussions and a focus on shifting mindset.

—Jennifer Ayers, Executive Director at Northwest High Performance Enterprise Consortium (NWHPEC)

Hospital operating room (OR) teams often have to delay their patient care work when they open a surgical pack to find some instruments are missing, broken, or dirty. This kicks off surgical pack rework loop — to quickly find replacements or do a quick sterilization (which is not as sterile as the full process done properly). Often, the first instinct is to try speeding up the rework cycles. It's more effective to reduce use of the rework cycle. The team found many ways to do so, including helping the OR team understand how (and why) to properly pre-clean instruments before sending them down to sterile processing. Improved standardized work helped reduce the number of missing or broken instruments. Reducing, if not eliminating, rework is the ideal solution for the benefit of patients, surgeons, and the hospital.

—Mark Graban, Author of books including *Lean Hospitals* and *Measures of Success*

> Rework is paying double salaries to produce an inferior product at the expense of machine time and output of quality product.
>
> —Karen Ginsbury, Owner of PCI Pharmaceutical Consulting Israel, Ltd.

REFLECTIONS

You may be familiar with clients who create Standard Operating Procedures (SOPs) for rework loops. Even if they realize they have to address the rework, teams consider themselves too busy working the backlog to entertain the possibility of a permanent fix. It requires a pause and permission to stop working "in" the process briefly while working "on" it toward a long-term gain. It helps if you push against the idea that it's normal to do things twice.

INK MAKES YOU THINK

Think of a time you've seen colleagues grow accustomed to honing and perfecting rework.

- Who might be open to putting an end to the rework?
- What would you ask them?
- What do you think they'll say?

7

DIG THE BEST PATH TO ROOT CAUSE

WHERE ARE YOU LOOKING FOR ANSWERS?

WHERE ARE YOU LOOKING FOR ANSWERS?

There's an old joke: A man outside of a bar is searching under a streetlight for his car keys. A patron leaving the bar sees him, and joins him in his search for the keys under the lamp.

After having covered what seems like every inch of the area, the patron asks, "Are you sure this is where you lost them?" The man reflects for a moment. "No, but the light is much better here."

The thing that generally makes jokes funny is the grain of truth. The *grain* here is the human inclination to go the easy route. How does that show up in the problem-solving world? Searching for root causes where it's easy as opposed to considering where you should be looking. Are you investigating by talking to a work buddy instead of others who might know more about the issue? Are you studying an old Standard Operating Procedure instead of watching how people do the work? There's also the issue that existing data may not be as helpful as it needs to be.

One team lead was trying to understand the reasons so many insurance claims required manual adjustments. Luckily, claims adjusters had to document the reason for each adjustment. The system had a drop-down list to choose from. Unfortunately, it offered seventeen choices and 80% of the responses were "other." In that case there was data, but it wasn't *useful* data.

More often than not, data isn't waiting to be discovered in a system. There are still options. The first is going to where the work happens to listen, observe, and talk to people. One team lead was convinced that nurses were not properly updating a required form because they didn't consider it important—it seemed obvious. After a visit to the facility, she was struck by how many phones were ringing and how distracting it was. It took time out of her day, but what she learned was invaluable.

Then there's the option of manually collecting data. For those new to formal problem solving, that may not enter their minds as an option. Data? How would I get it? That's something computers generate. I have no time for that. But it could be a simple sheet of paper with some check marks. One team leader knew that people were struggling to find supplies. After considering how to measure the "baseline," he posted a sheet requesting sign-in and sign-out times outside the storage facility. The length of time people spent in the facility gave him his baseline.

A common root cause is "lack of training" and the immediate question is "what don't they know?" If there's a knowledge gap, how would you verify that? One team leader devised a simple knowledge check survey and gave it to the staff. It allowed her to establish the exact information they were missing. Once she developed her solutions, she used the survey again to check if she'd filled the gap. Surveys are subjective but she used hers to clarify the extent of the gap and the type of missing information. They helped with root cause *and* countermeasures.

If people are searching for root causes where it's easy, rather than where they could discover the truth, they might need support and permission to step back and reassess.

There are generally no street lamps exactly where people need them, but others can help light the way.

———

The Wisdom of the Crowd—How do you help people focus their root-cause analysis?

> I have coached problem solvers to conduct experiments to see if a cause is truly a cause. For example:
>
> Problem: The customer doesn't complete the form needed to request services.

Cause Identified: The customer doesn't know about the form.

Solution: Communicate to customers about the form.

Experiment: Measure the results. If nothing changes, you can eliminate this as a cause and explore the additional causes.

—Hollie Jensen, Director of Strategy & Performance Improvement at Alaska Airlines

Formal problem solving is not our natural path. It's not something we get exposed to in school, which is where we're taught to focus on getting the right answer quickly. We tend to skip the hard work of understanding the true nature of the problem—what it is, exactly. And we tend to rush our analysis of what is causing it in our haste to find a solution. The trick is to keep asking questions. "How do we know it's a problem?" "How do we know we've found the root cause?" "How do we know we've got the best alternative to try?"

—Hugh Alley, Author of *Becoming the Supervisor*

As simple as it is, I always start by asking, 'What is the problem we are trying to solve?' So often we want to jump right to solutions, but a well-defined problem, as they say, is a problem half solved. Conducting that initial diagnosis to get the problem well-documented is key. Then we can move to our 5 Whys (asking "why" until you get to the root of an issue).

—Leslie Henckler, Business Design and Transformation at TriNet

REFLECTIONS

Root cause analysis is the crux of formal problem solving but it's not necessarily a natural path. If we've made it past the "jumping to solution" phase, we still have to help them stick the landing in the analysis phase. The trick is to keep asking questions. "How do you know that's the root cause?" See what they say.

INK MAKES YOU THINK

- What is one question you could ask those you work with to help them dig to the root cause?
- Ask the next problem solver who's searching under a streetlamp.
- What do you think will happen when you ask?

8

QUESTION THE PROCESS BEFORE AUTOMATING IT

AUTOMATE IT!

It's hard to imagine any process that wouldn't benefit from automation. The trick is the approach.

A project leader hit a familiar snag. Her only countermeasure was automation, but her IT ticket had been in the queue for over a month. Since it wasn't an emergency, she was unclear when they'd get to it.

She was stuck in limbo, unable to show any progress, and disillusioned. She was trying to reduce defects in a hospital equipment rental process. After asking what she'd discovered in terms of the root causes she offered, "It's missing credit card information. I spend hours trying to reach patients. I am constantly chasing down the info. Then I edit the rental contracts so the hospital can get paid. I'm the rework loop."

Her solution to create an automated sign-up process sounded reasonable, but she wanted to try improving the process in the meantime. Could she address that issue in a low- or no-tech way? She said, "Part of the current process is for me to leave a printed stack of contracts at the gift shop. What if I used a yellow marker to highlight the credit card area that they often leave blank? It wouldn't take much time for me to add a little visual guidance to the form. It's not completely mistake-proof, but if it cuts down on the time I waste running around after people, that's a win." She sounded energized.

She conducted her interim solution and cut her rework by half. As a result of what she learned, she edited her request for the IT department to make the credit information come earlier in the process and make the right fields mandatory. She also realized there was required information that no one was using so she revised her IT ticket to include only what the hospital needed for the automated sign-up.

There are lots of automation options that might help make a process run faster or reduce mistakes, and there are a few steps to take before it can happen. One step is to truly study the existing process in order to make sure it's ready for automation. Is everyone using their own spreadsheets to make something work? How do those become automated? Is there existing software to replace them, or would someone need to create new software? Sometimes automation is too big a leap, and the process requires rethinking to pave the way.

Another issue is that automation could be more illusion than solution. It's out of immediate reach for many team leads, like the one mentioned here, so they have no control over implementation. IT Departments receive a steady supply of requests, and they have to not only prioritize, but also ensure that implementing something new for one department won't have unintended consequences for another. They're in charge of risk assessment.

People also use digital transformation as a way to stave off problem solving,

"There's a system upgrade coming that should solve this, so we should wait." But the "wait" might be over a year, and waiting is a waste.

Problem solvers grow bored and move on. And when the upgrade appears, it often fails to solve the issue.

"Lack of automation" consistently comes up in the guise of a problem. When asked, "what will automation solve?" the true problems surface. Once you've clarified the problem, you can study the process to see what's causing the problem. If it's due to errors people are making upstream, will automation solve that? If the process takes too long because of approval delays, will automation take care of that?

Automation is definitely an option for solving some process issues, but it's not the place to start.

————

THE WISDOM OF THE CROWD

How do you deal with the assumption that automation is a cure-all?

> I have alligator arms (not long enough to reach into my pockets) which means I'm frugal. My old-school attitude defaults to the days before automation was seen as the answer which makes me ask, "Walk me through how this works. What are the inputs, outputs, and customer needs?" Essentially, 'prove it.' And because I'm cheap (frugal), I need to see a cost/benefit calculation to demonstrate that automation will help the trifecta (cost/quality/speed).
>
> —Jennifer Tankanow, Co-founder and VP of JointPivot

> Automation is as good as the process was before being automated.
>
> —Julie Savage-Fournier, Process Design and Process Improvement Consultant at Kaizen Radical

> One resource I've turned to repeatedly is the correct sequence for considering improvements: 1) Eliminate rework, 2) Address capacity issues, 3) Improve information in the workplace, 4) Improve flow, 5) Technology. I'm not positive about the source, but when I've cited this list, in order, it has helped senior management rethink automation.
>
> —Hugh Alley, Author of *Becoming the Supervisor*

REFLECTIONS

One of the reasons for the bias is that automation can provide the *perception* of improvement. It eliminates some waste such as motion and transportation so the process is quicker. But without conducting some form of analysis it might result in more or faster rework as the process is still producing errors. Automation can be a great answer, but it's key to encourage problem solvers to answer a few questions first.

INK MAKES YOU THINK

- Are you considering automation yourself?
- Is someone else recommending it?
- What experiment could you run to demonstrate that automation will make a difference, before you do it?

9

STAY OPEN TO NEW BEST WAYS

DO YOU SUFFER FROM BEING RIGHT?

DO YOU SUFFER FROM BEING RIGHT? MAYBE.

On the surface, the to-do list pictured is what it appears to be—outdoor chores for me and my husband. At first glance, it appears to be fulfilling its purpose since we are working through the list. Upon closer inspection it's domestic conflict. We'll come back to that, but there's always a potential for conflict when establishing the right way to do something.

There's an opportunity to establish the *current best way* to conduct a given task—to clarify and document the steps. But according to whom? You know it should be created by the people doing the work, but what if there's disagreement about the method? You know there's variation in how things happen in any process. Sometimes variation provides an opportunity to adapt and evolve, but there can be only one standard.

Back to the backyard battle. There's more than one way to execute a to-do list. We created the list in the morning as we strolled through the yard—a suburban *Process Walk*—or "Gemba Walk," using the Japanese since it's more fun to say. It's an informational walk through a process—where things are actually happening—to understand the issues and opportunities. While most process walks involve interacting with people, this one was more concerned with shrubberies. Still, dealing with the yard was a process.

Throughout the rest of the day, we referenced the list separately as we worked through the chores. It seemed obvious—to me—that given the blank square to the left of each task, "users" should add a checkmark inside the square to indicate a completed task. While glancing at the list on a break, it appeared my husband had simply crossed out entire line items.

It was insulting to see him ignore the stated plan, and his ungainly scrawl was obscuring the written tasks. You had to strain to tell exactly what we'd accomplished. There was no need to say anything since the list was essentially doing its job—we were getting things done. Plus, I know better. Was I still dying to enforce what I knew to be *the* best way to work the list? Yes. Yes I was.

After relaying this later to my husband, he pointed out that the two separate methods allowed us to see who did what. Sigh.

The issue is around developing the best way to do something. You are often working with colleagues to create or update the way things should be done. You may be responsible, but if you take on all the decisions around the outcome, you may get pushback.

People might cross out your fine work if they've had no say in the process. Invite others to join you when navigating the path to the new best way.

———

THE WISDOM OF THE CROWD

What are some examples of good guidelines you've used to help others come up with the *current best way*?

> We should explain the 'why' of the standards. For example, I don't like crossing out checklist items because some items repeat from one list to the other and I use the old checklist to verify if I've missed something. I need to be able to read the tasks even when they are completed. Also, we should never assume that something that makes sense for us makes sense for everyone.
>
> —Julie Savage-Fournier, Process Design and Process Improvement Consultant at Kaizen Radical

> In terms of establishing standards at home, my biggest frustration for years was when I asked the kids to do the dishes. I often found myself having to do a quality

control check, pointing out all the things they missed. Eventually I got smart. I sat the kids down, borrowed an Agile concept and had them create a 'Definition of Done' for what 'Doing the Dishes' meant. When we all agreed that their list looked good, that became the standard. When I did a quality check after that, there was no more arguing about what 'done' looked like, I simply asked them if this met their definition of done and if not, they knew what they needed to do because they had defined it themselves.

—Jared Thatcher, Author of *Parenting the Lean Way*, and Host of the Virtual Lean Summit

During our 2017 Aviation Resource Management Survey (ARMS), I drafted the *perfect* Pre-Accident Plan (PAP). During the inspector's review he told us we had passed—however—we had glaring gaps! The inspector made the point that although we developed a great product, it was only useful to people who understood Aviation Safety incursions—not the personnel in our flight operations section. He recommended we revise the PAP to incorporate the end user. Ask the question "How would you do this?" or "Does this section make sense to you?" Having a standard is great, but you need to include others in creating it. If no one understands or knows how to employ it, it serves no one.

—Emilio Natalio, Chief of Staff with Resilience-Building Leader Program

REFLECTIONS

There are a few things at work here: the perils of bringing work concepts into the home, and the process of deciding on the best way to do something. The battle over the list of chores was laughable (eventually ...), yet it highlighted the need to work toward consensus on a process. What's the goal? What's your reasoning behind your preferences? And, most important, what does everyone else think? The phrase belies my affection for the furry buggers but, there's more than one way to skin a cat. Figure out what works—for everyone.

INK MAKES YOU THINK

- Imagine a colleague who has ingrained ideas about how a given process should be executed that you or others are not following.
- What's a good question to ask to help determine the better process?
- Or is it you who's growing frustrated with others not following your method?
- What could you ask to understand why?

10

USE SURVEYS WISELY

PROCESS VS. SURVEYS—CAN YOU BASE AN IMPROVEMENT EFFORT ON SURVEY RESULTS? SHOULD YOU?

I was recently coaching a nurse who wanted to improve a hospital's rating on patient sleep quality. It was one of the areas where they'd gotten low scores on their customer satisfaction survey. It was negatively impacting the patient experience. A worthy cause—but it brought up a few questions.

"What process would you be improving?" I asked. She mentioned all the beeps the equipment made, and she thought alarms probably kept people up, so she could study the equipment settings. Another issue might be how noisy things could be in the hallway, so she could potentially study the flow of staff. Her impression was that noise impacted a patient's ability to sleep. That made sense. How many of us have gotten a good night's sleep in a hospital?

I asked what she might measure. She thought the survey stats would be the baseline. Would that work? Surveys are subjective. Was there a more tangible thing to measure? She could measure the number of alarms that went off. If she could reduce that number she thought their scores would improve. That brought up another question, what kind of control would she have over reducing or removing alarms and other sources of noise? Alarms might be involved in essential aspects of healthcare.

I could see my questions were deflating and she seemed frustrated. She said her manager really wanted her to tackle this problem since the survey results were a sore point for the facility. I asked her to think about which process she could study, and something tangible she might measure, and we'd talk again.

At our next meeting she had a better idea of where to focus. She had gone to the facility and talked with patients themselves. Instead of alarms, she discovered it was the staff who disrupted their sleep by waking them up. She knew sometimes they woke people to give them medications, and sometimes they woke them just to check on them at the end of a shift. She'd have to dig more. She was happy she spent the time with patients. She switched her project to focus on the process of staff visiting patients, and the number of times they woke patients up.

It's hard to convince people that customer surveys might not make the best baseline for an improvement effort. We often refer to them as "smile sheets." Likert scales seem to add rigor, but even if you use numbers, they're based on perception. As an example, "On a scale of 1 to 7, how do you feel about your experience?" This turns impressions into a number. Maybe you've got a headache coming on so, you give it a "2." It's a personal translation as opposed to a true process measure.

Surveys are also "lagging" indicators. They take a volume of perceptions and emotions and bundle them together after the fact. What led to those responses? What was happening in those moments? How do you tease out what processes were involved? It's hard to bank an improvement effort on moving the survey needle. The nurse was hoping to see a shift in the survey, and talking to the patients helped her pick something to study and measure.

Surveys are a great place for problem solvers to start. They alert you to troubling issues, and qualitative scales can peg the severity of any given problem. But knowing *that* people are dissatisfied is not the same as knowing *why*. A low score on a satisfaction survey could mean many things. You need to encourage those you work with to establish what lies *beneath* the scores before they can use them to guide their efforts.

———

THE WISDOM OF THE CROWD

What are some good ways you've found to help others address poor survey scores using process improvement?

I am a big advocate of surveys, but with the caveats that you raise. They can tell you that you have a problem, even if they don't tell you a lot about what the problem is. The flip side? A lot of surveys are the problem that needs to be solved! Double-barreled questions, questions that presume to know the needs of the customer, etc.

—Steven Thomson, PhD, Lean Consultant

It is always important to capture the voice of the customer. However, surveys are dangerous in that there are so many ways for them to go wrong. The data needs to be continuous (I prefer 1-10 scales). The pool of participants in the survey need to be both random and representative of the larger population. The questions, if not formed properly, can actually lead to predictable or controllable answers. There are other external variables that could cloud survey results, such as when questions are asked. Altogether, surveys can be great, but there are many opportunities to misinform. Altogether, I don't think that it is an either/or when it comes to process vs. surveys. It is both. However, surveys require extreme care.

—Dwight Harris, Jr. Dwight Harris, Jr., MBA, MBB, MS, CIRA, and Author of *Eliminating the Risk of Risk*

We push people to have a measurable entity for their improvement project, and satisfaction indexes/scores become a common candidate. But as you have stated, these metrics are a combination of a variety of causes and it's difficult to unbundle them in order to pursue an improvement effort. They are convenient measures (relatively easy to obtain), but leave the project without focus. Better to find the focal point at the beginning of the project rather than find you lack focus once you arrive at the Analyze Phase.

—Craig Tickel, Senior Consultant at Kaizen Institute

REFLECTIONS

Problem solvers need more than a survey to base an improvement effort on. The survey itself might not pass muster, and regardless of the quality of the questionnaire, you should encourage them to go and talk to the people who took the survey to discover the real experience behind their ratings. Surveys can be a good start, but they are just the beginning.

INK MAKES YOU THINK

- Are you, or people you work with, looking to hang your hats on moving the survey needle?
- What process would you or they be fixing?
- Who would be best to talk to in order to better understand the specific process pain?

CONSIDER YOUR ACTIONS—LOOKING BACK

Part One

We are all problem solvers, and we're responsible for encouraging the efforts of those around us.

Do you struggle with how to encourage people to broaden their thinking? You need to ask good questions, you need to tell thought-provoking stories, and you need to let people struggle. Are you concerned that redirecting people's temptation to jump to a solution will put a damper on their enthusiasm? What's key is how you do it. It's not enough to dictate what works.

Reflect on what you want to change about guiding those you work with. Do you have new questions to ask? Are you watching out for tripwires like "lack of" when someone describes a problem? It could be something as small as asking, "Have you spoken to any customers?" The potholes will always be there, you simply need to clarify the detours.

KEY POINTS SUMMARY

1. Let the Structure Set You Free
Limitations paradoxically free people up to innovate.

2. Listen, Customers are Talking
Going to where the work happens is the great assumption buster.

3. Clarify the Problem
If training didn't work the first time, retraining is unlikely to solve the problem.

4. Beware the Lure of the Quick Fix
People have been trained to jump to a solution—you can encourage true problem solving by clarifying the problem before experimenting to find solutions.

5. Share the Underlying Purpose
People are more vested in solving problems if they understand *why* they're doing it.

6. Do It Right—Don't Do It Over
Rework becomes an accepted way of operating if you don't challenge its reason to exist.

7. Dig the Right Path to Root Cause
Are people looking for answers where it's easy or have they considered all the options?

8. Question the Process Before Automating It
Automation is an increasingly attractive panacea—but is the process ready for primetime?

9. Stay Open to New Best Ways
People's attachment to their own ideas can stall innovation.

10. Use Surveys Wisely
Surveys are good starting points. Keep in mind that they fall short on the "whats" and "whys" behind the responses.

UP NEXT

As you work to develop yourself and those you work with, how you communicate can make the difference between compliance and enlightenment. With experience comes "the curse of knowledge." You've seen things. You know stuff. And you forget the other people don't. But that doesn't mean you impart what you know in a series of brain dumps. How you talk, text, email, post, and relay your thoughts to others makes a difference. Time to consider how to be a better communicator.

Part Two

SPEAK THOUGHTFULLY

What you say matters. How you say it matters, too.

As you gain experience, you've got more to say. Paradoxically, knowing *more* means it might be time to consider saying *less*. Maybe your delivery is in transition from less telling to more asking. Either way, there's often a gap between what we *plan* to say and what comes out. When you're rushing to meet deadlines and get things done, you might be too stressed to care—yet that's when your words make the most difference.

There are endless personality assessments out there—Meyers-Briggs, DISC, Hogan, and so on. Yes, it is good to know yourself better, and there are also some simple truths about communication regardless of the designations you receive from any of these assessments. How you speak to others influences what they hear. The words you use, and the questions you ask, can provide clarity or leave people feeling lost. The good news is that there are simple ways to approach both the written and spoken word that make a big difference.

11. Beware the Illusion of Listening
Are you simply waiting to talk?

12. Get Curious About Conflict
Resist the urge to guess people's motives.

13. Invite People Into the Change Process
Have you truly included others?

14. Remove Blame from the Room
What kind of example are you setting?

15. Use Your Words
Manage the role of jargon in creating barriers.

16. Spell It Out
Just say no to acronyms and the Tower of Babel.

17. Absorb and Harness Input
Are you able to take in helpful feedback?

18. Show People You Care
Modeling empathy and humility enhances the culture.

19. Make Sure You're Understood
Avoid conflict by managing the methods of communication.

20. Give People Feedback They Can Hear
Use words to build and encourage others.

11

BEWARE THE ILLUSION OF LISTENING

THE OPPOSITE OF TALKING ISN'T LISTENING

THE OPPOSITE OF TALKING ISN'T LISTENING, IT'S WAITING TO TALK.

This truism comes from my colleague John Guaspari, author of *I Know It When I See It*. It highlights what's often happening during a conversation. One person is talking, and the other is busy working out what they'll say next. Listening is a casualty.

While working at a consulting firm early in my career, at some point it became obvious that all the principals had developed a strategic stammer. During discussions in the conference room, they wielded this stutter to maintain the floor, "I, I, I, was thinking … " They kept talking, even if it meant repeating themselves, as they formed their next point. They'd honed the stutter as a defensive maneuver to keep others from cutting in. They seemed instinctually aware that people were busy forming their responses and eager to speak. It was oratory as competition.

The technique reminded me of dinners with my family. There were often ten of us around the table so the trick to being heard was to have a good story. My stepfather was a masterful storyteller—his voice spun tales slowly and with such detail that he commanded all ears and eyes. No stutter required. Lacking his skills and low resonant voice left the rest of us at a disadvantage. To be heard over siblings you had to keep things interesting, or risk being interrupted. And just when you thought you'd hooked everyone, an older sister might jump in with a juicy tangent, and your story would be lost. Another defeat.

It's taken years to unlearn conversation as competition. It's taken even longer to let go of forming my next sentence while someone else is talking. It turns out our brain science is working against us. We can process what people are saying much faster than people can speak. And we form our own thoughts thousands of times faster than that. We're the only ones who can manage this high-speed thought train. We need to perform three roles, talker, listener, and discussion mediator.

It's especially hard if your current culture doesn't support active listening. In those organizations everyone is generally engaged in advocacy. The goal in those scenarios is to get your ideas out and be heard. All that advocacy without inquiry means there's no true exchange of ideas. Everybody loses.

One problem is defining our value by what we add to a conversation. With experience comes opinions. As you grow older and wiser, it stands to reason you've got more to offer. If you're being paid for your expertise, then people need to hear it! But what if you shift your perspective regarding *how* you add value? A well-crafted question can be a crucial catalyst. You must listen with the intent to understand in order to ask the right questions.

One "discussion mediation" technique you can use, when there are more than two people in the conversation, is to intervene when someone else gets cut off. Say something along the lines of, "I'd like to hear what [Person X] had to say." Or, even if they haven't been cut off, take a moment to invite them into the conversation. That way you get gems from the more contemplative of the group. You're also modeling active listening.

Listening is a lifelong pursuit.

———

THE WISDOM OF THE CROWD

How do you overcome the "waiting to talk" syndrome?

> But what if what I have to say is more interesting than what they're saying? I say that tongue in cheek of course, but this is often the thought process behind it. Of course, how do you know it's more interesting if you aren't really listening. To answer the question, when I'm coaching or advising I take notes. I almost never use the

notes, but it gives me something to do to focus me on what they are saying.

—Jamie Flinchbaugh, Author of *People Solve Problems*

One key is to set intention—in the moment and at a macro level. What is your purpose and impact you want to have? And what actions align with achieving it? I call this an 'intention pause'. Years ago, I realized I was unintentionally cutting people off with my ideas or not listening because I was thinking about what I was going to say next. My intention was to help the other person solve their problem, but my actions were not supporting this. To improve, I practiced the 'intention pause' by reminding myself of the impact I wanted to have. I stayed aware of wanting to interrupt and counted to 10 after asking a question. I refocused when I found myself not listening. It was hard, but with purposeful practice I got better over time!

—Katie Anderson, Leadership Consultant and Author of *Learning to Lead, Leading to Learn*

A life hack to catch yourself is to write the acronym W.A.I.T (Why Am I Talking?) at the top of your paper or notebook you're using. Also, I used to hide my self-view on Zoom, but now I keep it on. I catch visual cues of myself not listening, or frowning, eyes wandering, etc. There's something about truly believing in the value of listening. We—and by that, I mean me—have to unlearn the thought that you only add value by sharing your opinion.

—Dorsey Sherman, MHSA, ACC, and President of Modèle Consulting

REFLECTIONS

It could be the "intention pause" or the "clarity pause" but the first step to listening is to take a breath. The second step is to focus on understanding the other person. And the last point, even among professionals with lifelong training, is to keep practicing. To truly listen is not easy for anybody.

INK MAKES YOU THINK

- Do you find yourself waiting to talk?
- Are you guilty of more advocacy than inquiry?
- How might you make room for others?
- How do you think they'll respond?

12

GET CURIOUS ABOUT CONFLICT

ASSUME GOOD INTENT AND SEEK TO UNDERSTAND

ASSUME GOOD INTENT, AND SEEK TO UNDERSTAND. EASIER SAID THAN DONE.

I texted my colleague asking, "Did you review that article I sent you Friday? You know it's publishing tomorrow, right? I really need to hit that deadline." Hard not to miss my frustration. My assumption was that the answers were "no" and "no, I forgot." Hitting send was like sending a peeved flick of the fingers. Slightly righteous with some vague moral superiority. She texted back, "Of course! It looks awesome, I sent you a few suggestions. Didn't you get my response? I really like it!" Scanning my inbox, her email had inadvertently routed into spam. Okay then ... All. Good.

Jean Paul Sartre wrote, "Hell is other people." He maintained that the phrase has been misunderstood but it's easy to see why he's so widely quoted. People can be difficult. We construct organizations to pull people together and create something bigger than we could accomplish by ourselves. If we build solid systems and support blame-free cultures, then there's no limit to what we can do together. But sometimes we run afoul of each other. When things go wrong, we can become so infuriated we can't get anything done. We're too busy visualizing how to load the offender into a circus cannon.

Have you ever fired off an email basically asking, "What the ... ?!" And when your valued colleague responded you discovered your assumptions were wrong? Maybe you didn't completely read through what they sent and you missed something? You not only feel bad, you most likely look bad. Worse, it may take time and effort to repair the relationship. And if you copied anyone on the angry email it might take a good long while.

When something goes wrong, do you find yourself guessing at the motives of others? Assuming the worst? It's hard to resist thinking we know the "why" behind people's behavior. Going down this road generally leaves us emotionally hijacked. We can no longer focus on the job at hand. And there's more: we may be flat out wrong. If the situation escalates then we waste time and plans go off track.

What if we assume good intent? That frees us up to ask questions, to find out what's happening for the other person. That effort alone often serves to defuse a situation. What's key is starting from a positive stance. It's palpable and inviting. But not always easy.

My current technique when I find myself writing an angry email is to finish writing it. But then go back and search for the assumed "facts." Toss out the first email and craft questions to verify if the assumptions are true or not. Take the elements that feel *most* true, and preface them with a polite disclaimer, "I could easily be mistaken, but …" Inserting caveats does two things. The recipient is gently invited to set the record straight. If wrong, it's easy to move on with the right information. And if I'm right? Well, start loading the cannons.

If it makes it any easier, Napoleon, and several others are credited with saying, "Never attribute to malice that which is adequately explained by stupidity."

———

THE WISDOM OF THE CROWD

How do you resist assuming bad intent?

> Neuroscience research supports an 11-second pause to gentle the amygdala. To avoid 26-28 hours of cortisol running wild in our body. Over many coaching stories I have found people getting creative with this 11-second pause, like playing with Legos before going into a potentially intense meeting. It works!
>
> —Sunitha Narayanan, Leadership Impact Coach

> I'm taking my final coaching course and it's all about understanding when you are in 'Judger' (certain, judgmental) mindset and when you are in 'Learner' (curi-

ous, open, interested) mindset. I am trying to be more present as to when I am in one mindset vs. another and then asking, Do I want to be in Learner mode? Also, I try not to feel bad about feeling bad. There's nothing wrong with being angry, judgmental, or upset. It's natural. From there my practice is to get curious. What question or thought is causing this emotion? A lifelong practice! Based on amazing work from Marilee Adams.

—Dorsey Sherman, MHSA, ACC, and President of Modèle Consulting

When I feel myself assuming negative intent, I stop and count to 10 and breathe deeply. Then I get out a piece of paper and write down all the other possible reasons that the behavior is happening from the other person's point of view. Stopping the focus on myself, how I am feeling, and how I am affected, helps me most.

—Karyn Ross, Activator and Author of *The Kind Leader*

REFLECTIONS

The key is taking a moment before responding. In *My Stroke of Insight: A Brain Scientist's Personal Journey*[1], Dr. Jill Bolte Taylor describes the chemical response in our bodies when reacting to stressors in the environment. If we can wait it out, the full alert will pass and we operate more rationally. Everyone benefits from taking a step back and considering how they might bring the situation up with the goal of maintaining the relationship and resolving the conflict. Just like responding to the drivers who cut you off on the highway—if you fume and direct foul hand gestures into the air then you've become a distracted driver and the offender is long gone.

INK MAKES YOU THINK

- Think of a time when someone committed a perceived offense.
- Write down all the other possible explanations for the offending behavior.
- What is your perspective now?
- What questions might you ask?

---

1. Jill Bolt Taylor, *My Stroke of Insight: A Brain Scientist's Personal Journey*, (*Penguin Group, 2009*)

13

INVITE PEOPLE INTO THE CHANGE PROCESS

ARE YOU DOING IMPROVEMENT "TO" OR "WITH" PEOPLE?

The difference is big. Has anyone ever wiped out your elegant solution? Have you watched with disappointment as the "old" process reemerged? Have you ever been shocked that your improvement idea was rejected?

There are lots of reasons this happens, but one big one is that you may have missed a few conversations. Or maybe you did all the thinking and fixing on your own. Or you *did* involve others, but not *all* the "others." Your instincts might be good. Maybe you don't want to bother people. You're trying to make their lives easier. Regardless of the reason, it's disconcerting when the effort isn't appreciated. And even more disconcerting for the people who have to live with the unexpected change.

An entire team of nurses got together to reorganize the nursing station. They reimagined the space to make it easier to access information and find patient records. They were intensely proud of their work. And when the nursing night shift arrived, they saw the new setup and switched it all back before morning. The improvement team had neglected to include their colleagues. Frustration reigned on both sides.

A child development supervisor had a similarly aggravating experience while trying to reduce the number of incidents in her preschool classrooms. These incidents resulted in injured children, damaged property, and disrupted activities.

She had involved most of the teachers, observed their classrooms and worked with them to identify why the incidents happened. They realized the layout of the room was a major factor. Low bookshelves in the middle of the space served as launch pads for energetic kids. Large open spaces turned into high-speed racetracks. They experimented and discovered that creating separate nooks for reading and napping reduced the incidents. Kids ran around outside. They leapt and skipped rope—just not in the classroom.

Incidents dropped across the board, except for one classroom. The supervisor hadn't had time to work with that teacher, so she took it upon herself to move the furniture into the new layout for the classroom over the weekend to save time. When she visited the classroom, she saw that the teacher had returned to its original layout.

The rejection was demoralizing, and her initial instinct was to report the teacher to the administration. But she thought better of it. Instead, she reached out to the teacher and they agreed to reconsider a layout that would meet everyone's needs. They co-developed a new classroom design, and incidents dropped once again.

It's startling to see your good work undone. When it happens to you, you might consider that perhaps the other person found it equally disconcerting to find their workplace, workflow, or "stuff" disrupted. No one appreciates having improvement done "to" them.

———

THE WISDOM OF THE CROWD

How do you make sure you make improvements "with" people instead of "to" them?

> From a behavioral perspective, we look at improvements mostly from a task-flow lens when they are done 'to' people. However, the way tasks are done is not purely logical (even logic is subjective!). When we co-create, it takes care of the latent layers of convenience, habit, and preference in a safe zone. Just the fact that we have the option to say no, makes us more amenable to saying yes.
>
> —Dr. Sabiha Mumtaz, Assistant Professor at the University of Wollongong in Dubai

One of my early Lean teachers said, "It's uplifting to Kaizen (run a Rapid Improvement Event). It's trauma-tizing to be Kaizen'd!" Seared in my brain. Applies in life as well. Inclusion is the key.

—Karen Martin, Author of *Clarity First*

I use my Wheel of Sustainability to provide an image to leaders of their role in the improvement process. It helps them build and demonstrate the behaviors that support a team so that they can win. An example is an exchange to clarify benefits during a Kaizen (Rapid Improvement Event). This is where they go out, in the middle of developing their improvements, and share what they're thinking and why with others who aren't on the team. They do this one-to-one, and everyone comes back with high-value feedback and challenges. It's the reality check for how the organization will react and respond to the changes before it's too late.

—Adam Lawrence, Author of *The Wheel of Sustain-ability*

REFLECTIONS

This is a constant issue in all realms. Even in the face of seemingly helpful technology upgrades, people find manual workarounds or ways to stick with the old system, especially if they were not a part of the solution. One issue is how long people have been using the *old* way or system. Logic and common sense are no match for ingrained working patterns. By contrast, when the patterns of work are dictated to people, they have little incentive to help overcome the obstacles that inevitably arise.

INK MAKES YOU THINK

- Do you, or people you work with, tend to go it alone?
- What is a question that would encourage them (or you) to consider including other stakeholders?
- Who might you include?
- How do you think they'll respond?

The risks from failing to involve others are much greater than the risk of oversharing.

14

REMOVE BLAME FROM THE ROOM

DO PEOPLE EXPECT TO BE BLAMED?

DO PEOPLE EXPECT TO BE BLAMED? THE ANSWER IS YES MORE OFTEN THAN NOT.

While onsite with a Canadian client preparing to run a simulation with twenty-five managers, we discovered the pencils in the kit were unsharpened. I was puzzled and annoyed since the event was about to begin. It was a minor issue, but why would our staff pack unusable pencils?

It seemed like an easy fix to find enough writing implements for thirty people. The client let me know we were stationed at a relatively empty facility, and she had no access to supplies. She asked her assistant to give her a hand, so off he headed into the empty offices searching for pencils and sharpeners. Neither was in immediate supply but eventually he found an old-school pencil sharpener. He set up a mini-sharpening factory in the back to supply the participants. The event was a delayed success.

During our next company huddle, a new employee let everyone know he'd done the packing. He was still in his teens, and excited to be working in an internet startup. But during this meeting he looked crestfallen. While describing the client event, I let everyone know what went well and what we could do better—myself included. Our mantra was to surface and fix problems. When we got to the pencils, he began apologizing for packing them without sharpening them. He was sorry the simulation was delayed and felt bad about everyone having to scramble. He promised he wouldn't get it wrong again.

His sense of guilt gave me pause. I asked him to check the packing instructions for the simulation kit. "Did it say anything about sharpening the pencils before adding the boxes?" He checked and it didn't.

"Well then that's on us, and we need to add that step to the instructions." He was both surprised and relieved we didn't blame him. "Wow, that's an interesting way to look at it!" It's easy to forget that blame is more the more common cultural norm than the ideal of everyone feeling free surfacing problems to make the system better.

Your job is to reinforce the goal of a good system—not root out the guilty parties.

———

THE WISDOM OF THE CROWD

Do people expect to be blamed and what can you do to change that?

> Be slow to judge and fast to ask clarifying questions. Immediate finger pointing creates the mindset in people that they are usually wrong.
>
> —Kyle Kumpf, Management Coach at Kumpf Consulting Group

> The label printers for the packing station routinely failed and operators frequently had to reset them. The blame and complaints came rolling in, "These things suck ... Purchasing picked the cheapest thing they could find ... Maintenance won't ever do anything about it ... Management doesn't even care, they just want us to be busy all the time ... 'They' caused this problem ..."
>
> I wrote 'Mr. Process' on a sheet of paper and stuck it to the back of the chair. I challenged the team to think about this faulty printer as a broken process. We agreed that the root causes were depleted battery packs, insufficient charging cords, no resupply of batteries, no printer replacements in stock, etc. When the team saw the headache in this light, it was easy to rally together and get tough with Mr. Process!
>
> —Jesse DePriest, Vistage Chair, Lean Leadership and Transformation Coach

1. Is there a standard? 2. Did we follow the standard? 3. Did the standard produce a bad result? If the answer to the first question in this sequence is no, then all we have left is 'blame the person.' We can either blame the process or blame the person, but if there is no process, we end up blaming the person.

—Jamie Flinchbaugh, Author of *People Solve Problems*

REFLECTIONS

There is violent agreement on blame being the norm. Given how common it is, people tend to rush to their own judgments. For some, the answer is to deflect the blame onto others in anticipation. For others it's somehow less painful to fall on their own sword than to wait for someone else to wield the blade. What's key as a leader is to check for clarity first. Be a model of curiosity and work to ensure people have the information and ability to do their jobs.

INK MAKES YOU THINK

- Think of a current performance problem.
- What question could you ask to determine if the person has the information and tools they need?
- What do you expect them to say?

Start there the next time something goes wrong.

15

USE YOUR WORDS

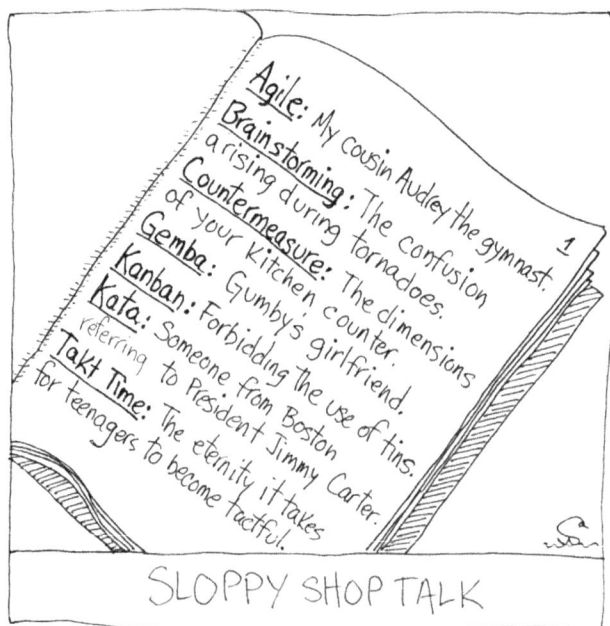

Agile: My cousin Audrey the gymnast.

Brainstorming: The confusion arising during tornadoes.

Countermeasure: The dimensions of your kitchen counter.

Gemba: Gumby's girlfriend.

Kanban: Forbidding the use of tins.

Kata: Someone from Boston referring to President Jimmy Carter.

Takt Time: The eternity it takes for teenagers to become tactful.

1

SLOPPY SHOP TALK

DO YOU ENGAGE IN SLOPPY SHOP TALK? DO YOU USE BUSINESS JARGON OR FOREIGN WORDS? SHOULD YOU?

Like other spheres, the continuous improvement world is rife with its own terminology. Some words are fun to say like the Japanese word, "Gemba" which translates to "the real place." It's more fun for me to talk about taking a "Gemba Walk" to see what's happening in the workplace. Better than the more sanitized "Process Walk." But then I have to explain myself. Maybe not—but I can't be sure if everyone knows what that means.

There are several attractive Japanese words, like "Hansei" and "Kaizen." Hansei means "reflection" which is worth translating since there can be precious little of that in our culture. What about "Kaizen"—a calming tea? No, it's a rapid improvement event. For anyone new to the concepts, it's initially gibberish.

We are in danger of producing the *Tower of Babel* effect. In the original story from the book of Genesis, when the workers began speaking different languages, they could no longer understand each other and were unable to finish the tower. Like building a tower, it's important to consider the work you're trying to accomplish, and the impact of new terminology. What obstacles might you be unintentionally creating to thwart the work at hand?

Every department in every industry is probably guilty of crafting its own language. The terms serve a purpose and they're often inventive. Logistics has "pups" which are half-sized containers hauled by tractors. "Bumping" within Human Resources means offering senior employees the option of taking other positions instead of being eliminated. If you're talking about a "dead cat" with radio types, you're referring to the fuzzy covering on a microphone. Combine that with using a "shotgun"—a long microphone—with the wrong audience and you could land in some serious trouble.

Each of these specialized lingos require mastery. Having to learn new words can set the bar higher than it needs to be. It can also lead to cultural barriers. Creating distinct vocabulary "camps" in an organization leads to verbal silos. People become separated based on whether they speak the language or not. Hearing foreign words can be alienating, and they signal that you're not part of the clique that understands them.

Forming distinctive vocabularies is a cross-industry phenomenon. A separate vocabulary might be warranted, but it pays to be strategic about your introduction. Not everyone will ask you to explain or define what you're talking about which means some will remain confused and less likely to participate. Reflect on the goal and whether it requires new terminology. Then use it sparingly.

———

THE WISDOM OF THE CROWD

How do you handle the Tower of Babel effect?

> When I work with organizations, I ask them to create terms and language that work for them and resonate with their purpose and the work they do. In general, when we create things, including words, we are more likely to have a shared understanding of what they mean, which makes us more likely to use them. For instance, my friends at Hennig call their Daily Standup Meetings, 'Daily Success Meetings' because their mission is, 'Making Our Customers Successful'!

—Karyn Ross, Activator and Author of *The Kind Leader*

> In general, I use jargon to communicate clearly with my peers. This is to avoid misunderstanding. I use a different language when speaking to my team. This is also to avoid misunderstanding. But foreign words, especially Japanese words, are sometimes used to

create and reinforce in-group/out-group dynamics. Which is basically the opposite of Lean philosophy. We have to maintain the emotional intelligence to meet and speak with people where they are, while making an effort not to put stumbling blocks in their way.

—John Thacker, Operational Excellence Coach and Host of *A Quality Podcast*

" When I taught a six-month problem-solving course, I gave everyone a manual that had a blank page for each section titled 'jargon.' We kept a flip chart up that said "jargon alert." We encouraged anyone to tell us any words that were unfamiliar to them, and we would write the word and definition. We tried to keep the language free of it, but you can never predict what words people understand.

—Stephanie Hill, Owner of Lightbulb Moment Consulting

REFLECTIONS

There are traditionalists who prefer the original language of a method like Lean because translations don't do it justice, but most people appreciate simple terms that demystify. The compromise is to include translations when using foreign terms or jargon. The goal is to keep insider lingo from turning the area of improvement into a unique club. If you want to include everyone, use terms that work.

INK MAKES YOU THINK

- When was the last time you checked if your colleagues knew what you're talking about?
- How might you check for understanding?

- What are some terms or concepts that might be eluding people?
- How might you create more clarity?

16

SPELL IT OUT

FUN WITH ACRONYMS   2

Introductory acronym list:

ADKAR: The act of buying a second automobile

ASAP: Description of a person, a sap, responding to a rush order

DEI: God of dice

SIPOC: Son of Spock

VUCA: Sound of a cat coughing up a hairball

WHAT DO THEY MEAN?

HEADING OFF THE HEADSCRATCHERS

HEADING OFF THE HEADSCRATCHERS—IN THIS CASE ACRONYMS.

Do you ever find yourself pausing when reading an acronym—deciphering what it means? Has anyone ever asked you to define an acronym you're using, and you can't remember the original words? CVS is a national pharmacy chain. Any idea what CVS stands for?

Acronyms seem efficient but they're counterintuitive. You shorten long words into initials to save time. You lessen your workload, but the person reading now bears the burden of translation. Is "CD" a certificate of deposit, compact disc, or constructive discontent?

When we meet people from different organizations, we exchange acronyms and decode them for each other. We disconnect from colleagues by forming silos, and part of what separates us is our private language of acronyms. Texting makes it worse. LOL.

They also remove meaning. While working with CVS a while back (it stands for Customer Value Stores, in case you're interested), they added the word "Health" after their initials because they wanted to connect their name with their purpose—"Helping people on their path to better health." Initials fail to inspire.

Acronyms work if you know what they mean. Once you know, you assume everyone does—remember the curse of knowledge. If not, and you're brave, you ask someone to translate. But asking takes time on both ends. At some point, you forget what they stand for, like CVS.

Acronyms make the most sense in places like the military or emergency rooms where memorizing shorthand speeds communication and saves lives. In other workplaces, acronyms might ease some communication, but they facilitate the creation of silos and pose challenges for new employees.

Enlightened companies create internal "wikis" (collaborative informational websites) to help employees decipher the organization's specialized language of initials. You've written acronyms on flip charts. You've asked about them in meetings. You've skipped past them in articles, posts, and books. They're here to stay, so make it a habit to clarify what they mean.

———

THE WISDOM OF THE CROWD

They seem unavoidable, so how do you deal best with acronyms?

> I used to have a boss in the Army that when somebody put an acronym on a slide during a briefing he went around the room. If somebody didn't know what it meant, the person who used it had to stand for the remainder of the meeting. Amazing how quickly acronyms started coming off slides.
>
> —Shane Wentz, CEO and Lead Consultant at Change in Latitude Consulting

> When I facilitate an outside group, I don't stop them from using acronyms, but I do question them and ask them to define them. I also have them spell them out on sticky notes. I'm quick at picking up languages, so for me an acronym is just another foreign word to learn and add to my vocabulary.
>
> —Jared Thatcher, Author of *Parenting the Lean Way* and Host of the Virtual Lean Summit

> I remember being shocked when I saw a colleague refer to an 'FU Meeting' until they clarified that it was their shorthand for Follow-Up.
>
> —Mark Graban, Author of books including *Lean Hospitals* and *Measures of Success*

REFLECTIONS

Acronyms drive the need for customized reference guides. They are often part of in-jokes or they result in bemused resignation. You can form a habit of spelling out acronyms when you use them. You can make it a habit to ask for acronym translations during meetings, in spite of appearing ignorant, so others see that as a norm. You can create and maintain searchable shorthand lists. Spelling things out may seem old school—but it's a little gift of clarity that somebody somewhere appreciates.

INK MAKES YOU THINK

- How do you handle acronyms?
- What do you do when you see one you don't understand?
- Want to change that?
- What is one thing to try the next time you're dealing with acronyms?

One small step for humankind.

17

ABSORB AND HARNESS INPUT

"NOTHING PERSONAL, BUT..."

"IT'S NOTHING PERSONAL, BUT ..."

Can you feel the hairs raising on the back of your neck? If you've heard that phrase before, you'd be human to suspect the opposite—oh, it's personal. Even without that particular phrase, the input might feel like an implicit attack. Not all feedback comes with this disclaimer, but it still might be tough to hear.

Early on in my career I arrived at work to find a sticky note on my desk that read, "See Me." I was working with a senior consultant on a script for an industrial film. My stomach churned while walking to his office. There was a cartoon caption over my head with a shaky-cam effect saying, "This can't be good." Turns out he simply wanted to talk about the script. He had no idea his note had become a harbinger of doom. That misplaced sense of terror seems almost comical, and yet, every so often ...

It's hard to separate ourselves from what we do, what we create, and what we think. When we hear the observations of others, they can feel like judgements about our character, our intelligence, or who we are as people. Especially if we are dedicated to our craft. What makes us great at our jobs makes it hard to listen to alternate takes.

If you stay detached, it's easier to hear feedback (let's be frank—criticism). But that's the opposite of engagement which is the hallmark of an accomplished leader. If you bring your unique self to what you do —if you add your special sauce—then your first reaction to feedback is bound to be defensive. It's like fending off a body blow. The amygdala is most likely heavily involved in this exchange. It's busy exporting cortisol and adrenaline to jack up our heart rates and boost our energy levels so we can fend off the threat of reproach. Imagine the emotional aftermath—wounded feelings and bruised egos strewn across the battlefield.

If you consider the situation rationally, you want to be able to hear what people have to say. As lifelong learners, part of the growing experience is to explore and refine who you are and what you do. You can be energized by discoveries that come from others—if you're open to them. Sometimes it requires time and reflection to take in new ideas. But those can lead to leaps in understanding and essential shifts in perspective. Those are truly gifts.

There's a phrase that captures that urge to reject unwanted input, "Feedback is a gift, feel free to re-gift it." It's funny because it contains the essential modicum of truth. Maybe you see the feedback as an ice bucket, or a scarf. Once you've passed it along, and your protective armor is in place, you might think you're safe from conflicting views. But if you don't accept the gift, on some level, you might miss out. The ice bucket may have come in handy entertaining new friends. The scarf could have kept you warm. The same goes for those you work with. It's your job to model what it looks like to absorb and grow from feedback.

———

THE WISDOM OF THE CROWD

How do you avoid taking things personally?

> You don't. It's okay to take things personally but keep excessive emotionality out of the equation—especially at work. Most of the time when I hear people at clients say, 'She (or he) takes things so personally!' or they say it directly to someone, I remind them that 'work *is* personal. If it wasn't personal, you'd have a workforce of apathetic robots.' But—there's a way to respond to feedback that's from a place of curiosity and a desire to grow and develop vs. being defensive.

—Karen Martin, Author of *Clarity First*

> I like to collaborate with others on work so that it's not *my* work but *our* work. We can give feedback to each

other and any feedback from outside is diffused across two or more people—less personal!

—Ken Eakin, Author of *Office Lean*

I am more open to 'correcting' or critical feedback from someone who also gives reinforcing feedback. If they are more aware of the full picture of what's going on, they pay attention, and they care about me. I love it when people ask for permission before giving feedback. As a receiver, I get to answer that question. And my answer might be, "No" or, "Not now," or I might ask, "What do you hope the outcome will be in sharing feedback?" or some version of that.

—Jamie V. Parker, Host of the podcast, *Lean Leadership for Ops Managers*

REFLECTIONS

What helps is not to remove emotion but honor it. And honor the person who summoned the courage to speak up. Feedback is meaningful for personal growth, but equally significant is who's giving the feedback and how they're doing it. Ultimately, it's up to you to take in what helps you and treat the rest as noise. It's not easy, but it might help to consider that others are watching and learning from your approach.

INK MAKES YOU THINK

- Do you want to get better at receiving feedback?
- Would you like to model for others what that looks like?
- What is one technique you'd like to?

18

SHOW PEOPLE YOU CARE

WALKING IN SOMEONE ELSE'S SHOES

WALKING IN SOMEONE ELSE'S SHOES REFERS TO THE IDIOM, "BEFORE YOU JUDGE A MAN, WALK A MILE IN HIS SHOES."

There are different versions of the phrase, yet the message remains a plea for empathy. Empathy refers to being sensitive to the feelings of others, and it requires capacity. Unfortunately, we don't always act with capacity.

My complaint was valid, but should I have sent it? We get the paper delivered daily and it's generally there in time for coffee with my husband. The weekend, on the other hand, has been a crapshoot. It's worth checking the driveway every half hour to see if it's lodged in a bush. Luckily the corner market stocks them if there's no sign of the paper by midday.

Composing a letter to the delivery woman took place in my head. She should know that Sunday is *the* day to sit and enjoy the paper. Unlike the bustle of the weekdays, Sunday brings full-color comics, time to read articles start to finish, and linger with the crossword. It's part of the marriage. Without a paper, the twenty-year routine goes off kilter.

She occasionally adds envelopes for tips. That request rankled a bit, so asking my husband to include a note about the late papers seemed appropriate. Did she realize that having a late Sunday paper was a problem? One day she inserted a message instead of an envelope. She wanted to let us know that her terminally ill husband had passed away. She apologized for the year of erratic deliveries and promised things would get better. She asked only that we text her instead of calling the company to complain as some had done. She wanted a chance to respond, and she needed the job.

My heart was in my throat. How difficult life had been for her. How crushing. Thankfully my husband never wrote that note. We were both relieved, but stepping back, is that a good rule? Not burdening this newly widowed mother was a good thing, yet alerting people to issues is not, in general, a bad thing.

You should be able to acknowledge problems, and there are better and worse ways to do it. Language and method matter. It's impossible to know all of a person's story, so it's worth asking. Without their story, you only have the tales you tell yourself which can make kindness tougher. The sooner you ask, the easier it is to address a problem.

––––––

THE WISDOM OF THE CROWD

How do you address issues with kindness?

> It's easy to say but tougher to do. Starting out with the question, 'Is everything ok?' has helped me in more than one situation of this kind. Either the person opens up and shares something you may not know, or they might say, "Everything is fine, why do you ask?" Which allows me to share my observation that Sunday deliveries are very hit and miss. And it is less likely to cause a defensive response.
>
> —Anton McBurnie, Founder and Managing Partner of CoSuccess Consulting® Inc.

> One idea is to learn not to take offense. That means; suspend judgment, listen, and extend kindness. As you discovered, there is usually (always?) more to the story. Said differently, how we respond to the perceived offense is a moment of truth—and there's freedom when we take the position that it's not about us.
>
> —Mark Halmrast, Business Consultant

> I can relate to the high emotions one feels when jumping to conclusions without getting the whole story.

I was introduced to the book *Loving What Is,* and I have had some wonderful takeaways. The first thing I do before my mind starts weaving pieces of information into a story is ask, "Is that true?" If my mind still says, "Of course it's true," then I ask myself "Can you *absolutely* know it's true?" Most times I am left with a feeling of gratitude for having managed to slow down my thinking (or story writing) ability. I still have a way to go but I am getting better.

—Raaghavan Venkatram, Lean Thinker

REFLECTIONS

As in so many situations, starting with curiosity makes the difference. It diverts the impulse to complain and opens the door to understanding. There are moments when people might mistake compassion for weakness and take advantage. But it's worth the occasional negative experience to cultivate empathy and humility. Those are always wider doors.

INK MAKES YOU THINK

- What is a current problem that's bugging you?
- Are you ready to file a complaint (whether real or imagined)?
- If it's a situation where you could find out the backstory, what would you ask?

It might be a particular situation, or you might turn it into a "go-to" question for when issues arise.

19

MAKE SURE YOU'RE UNDERSTOOD

ARE YOU KIDDING?

"ARE YOU KIDDING?"

That thought runs through my head more often than I'd like it too. A colleague was recently explaining to me how and where to upload some instructions—he was telling me about the old process which we'd updated. There was no room to interject, and it was frustrating to listen knowing he was wrong. My patience was wafer thin and, when I was finally able to set him straight, it probably wasn't a pleasant experience for him. Those aren't proud moments.

"How do you *not* know this?!" Does this ever race through your mind when talking to a seemingly uninformed staff member, co-worker, or colleague? The information is right there. The situation is obvious and somehow they "didn't get the memo." Do you feel aggravated and then struggle to keep it from showing?

Frustration runs rampant as the person you're talking to reveals themselves to be (in your mind) clueless. You want to say, "We just talked about this." Or point out, "This is basic." Or remind them, "This came up during this morning's huddle." Do you have a poker face? If not, your disbelief is there for all to see.

Then what? The person may sense your exasperation and become quiet or defensive. The resulting conversation might be short or full of excuses. Or they may be oblivious to your disappointment and move on without any discussion. But what is the opportunity here? They may not "get it" for lots of reasons.

Maybe they're distracted. They might be preoccupied with something they see as more important. They may be overwhelmed. They may simply perceive things differently. Maybe they had a bad night, week, or month. Or maybe you're not looking at the same things. The options for communication have mushroomed, so one of the issues is how each person prefers to communicate.

Modern workplaces still use email, and there's the option of integrated team texting apps, walkie-talkie-style apps, and apps specifically for international teams to text and call. Texting has become almost old-school and "snail mail" is reserved for special occasions. A client who was trying to reduce the time to onboard new hires discovered that one obstacle was using email when candidates were far more comfortable with texting. Emails went unanswered because they went unseen.

What's the right response when what you want to say is, "Really??!!!" How do you make sure you bring people with you? How do you make information stick?

_____

The Wisdom of the Crowd

How do you react appropriately when you're frustrated with the seeming cluelessness of others?

> So often we observe this in our communication with teams. Our care providers, frontline clinicians, night-shifters, weekenders, break nurses, and travelers don't receive and respond to our emails at the speed of administrative teams. Their priority is direct patient care. Instead of, "I sent the emails X days ago," we go to Gemba (where the work is happening) and observe their environment. What if we meet them where they are? We can provide digital signage in physician/nurse lounges, or soft reminders at daily morning huddles. We can bridge the information gaps once we understand the rocks in their shoes.
>
> —Lily Angelocci, Head of Transformational Healthcare Team for UC San Diego Health

> A great point to remember here is that people key their emotions on what they perceive as your emotional

state. When you get frustrated, they may become frustrated. When you seem frantic, they may become frantic. When you become calm and practice humble inquiry, they follow your lead. Be an emotional thermostat! *You* control how *you* react to a set of circumstances.

—Chris Burnham, Host of *The Lean Leadership* podcast

One issue is overload. Once, for fun, I tracked the number of policy changes that came to me as a manager for implementation in a large administrative law organization. Sixty in one month. Three a day. Each one well intended and justifiable. But how could I possibly roll all those out to my staff and still have them do their work?

—Hugh Alley, Author of *Becoming the Supervisor*

REFLECTIONS

There are two lines of attack (so to speak) that apply to this situation. One references a foundational tenet of Lean, to "go see." That means that if you're expecting people to have or be able to access information, you should check out their work environment and what that looks like for them. The information might need to take different forms. The other aspect is your response. Counting to eleven gives you the critical maturity pause. If you take a deep breath and lead with curiosity, you've got a shot at getting somewhere good.

INK MAKES YOU THINK

- Are there times you get frustrated with people around you who don't seem to be aware of the current system?
- What's one way you could figure out why?
- What do you expect to find?

20

GIVE PEOPLE FEEDBACK THEY CAN HEAR

WE ARE CRITICAL THINKERS

WE ARE CRITICAL THINKERS. AND CRITICAL THINKING INVOLVES EVALUATION AND JUDGMENT.

"I know how to break that."

This was an observation from my 5-year-old nephew as he assessed his older brother's Lego construction. My sister and I laughed because it's true on many levels. We were all confident he could break it, and his declaration points out a distinctly human condition—our innate ability to see faults, failings, and shortcomings. We're trained to be critical thinkers, which means we excel at criticism. As in the case of my unfiltered nephew, it's the first place our brains go, but that doesn't mean it should be our lead.

Do you ever get the impression that your feedback wasn't well received? Someone asks for your opinion but seems not to take it in. Or they didn't ask for your opinion and, like my nephew, you led with perceived imperfections, and they rejected it. Honest feedback is hard to deliver. Sometimes it's easier to say nothing. But there are times people want and need to hear from you. They, like you, want to get better at what they do, and you might be able to help. But if you fail to start the conversation the right way, people often shut down and your words are lost.

You can go back almost a century to Dale Carnegie's iconic *How to Win Friends and Influence People* and take in his own practice to be "hearty in my approbation and lavish in my praise." That's reminiscent of the top slice of bread in the modern-day "Feedback Sandwich." You start with a plus—what someone did well. Then you deliver your concern—what they could do better. And you end on another plus. Sandwiches are generally good food, so that's a positive right there. It also pushes your critical mind to consider what you like about something, and that's instructive for all concerned.

But this "sandwich" might leave people with mixed messages, so it's important to get clarity up front with exactly what the feedback exchange is meant to accomplish. Honesty is often overrated. Not that you should be dishonest, but it's key to begin with your intentions. Take a few beats to determine if the person you're talking to is ready for feedback. Then get agreement on what you both hope to accomplish with your observations. Those steps will impact how you go about it.

We all know how to break things, but the real work is in building and maintaining relationships.

———

THE WISDOM OF THE CROWD

How do you deliver feedback without alienating people?

> I teach a model adapted from *Conversations Worth Having* by Cheri Torres and Jackie Stavros.
>
> Check in with yourself—what are your thoughts and feelings? What is your intention with this conversation? Is it positive?
>
> Describe facts. Describe impact on the self and the organization. Acknowledge how you have contributed to the situation. Ask for ideas for change.
>
> —Dorsey Sherman, MHSA, ACC, and President of Modèle Consulting

> I have had good success providing feedback using a coaching technique from Ken Blanchard: Connect-Focus-Activate-Review. A little planning before the conversation and a little reflection afterwards makes future conversations more effective. Ensure you are listening to learn, ask empathetic questions, connect with the person by sharing personal experiences

openly and honestly, and help to build self-assurance and confidence.

—Brad Matthies, Senior Manager of Product Development & Lean Six Sigma at Pitney Bowes

I basically use Kegan and Laheys[1], "Language of ongoing regard." I put it into practice with "What? So what? Now what?" "What?" starts with concrete experience and observations without filters of good vs. bad. "So what?" communicates the impact on me, and emphasizes my own personal experience of the situation. "Now what?" consists of suggested possibilities for moving forward.

—Aric Ho, Director of Operations - Office of Healthcare Equity at University of Washington

REFLECTIONS

There are a lot of feedback models to choose from, and the best ones begin with connecting and establishing context with the receiver. There are also simple guidelines like picking the right place and time and asking if the other person is ready to talk. The conversation should help maintain and build the relationship. Be prepared to help since growth starts with an opportunity to change.

INK MAKES YOU THINK

- What's one change you might like to try when delivering feedback?
- What does it sound like?
- What do you think will happen when you try it out?

---

[1]. link to Kegan and Lahey's work: https://www.steveforman.com/robert-kegan/

SPEAK THOUGHTFULLY—LOOKING BACK

Part Two

The Irish playwright George Bernard Shaw famously said, "The single biggest problem with communication is the illusion that it has taken place." And, given the current abundance of venues for us to converse with each other, the illusions have vexingly multiplied. Whether we have the luxury of face-to-face conversation, the next-best-thing on video, or we're limited to a few sentences in an app—words matter.

Beware of the anonymity that email and even texting offers. It helps to read difficult communications out loud to make sure it's something you really want to say. Considering the beginning, middle, and end of what you have to say should be a constant practice.

As a leader, or an aspiring leader, you're always modeling the way for others. Even if you're unaware of the influence you have, the words you use, when you use them, or choose not to, make a difference. What are you going to change? How will you experiment?

KEY POINTS SUMMARY

11. Beware The Illusion of Listening
It's tempting to frame your value in terms of the opinions you offer, but people often gain more from the questions you ask.

12. Get Curious About Conflict
It's unlikely you know the motives of others, unless they tell you, and even then you can't be sure.

13. Invite People into the Change Process
"I'll do it myself" might prove to be faster, but without collaborators you sacrifice acceptance.

14. Remove Blame from the Room
Assume that people expect to be blamed and work hard to ensure the focus starts with the process.

15. Use Your Words
Know the lingo, and use it sparingly. Remove verbal barriers that confuse people and turn them into outsiders.

16. Spell It Out
Treat acronyms as you would foreign words. Make it a rule to provide translations.

17. Absorb and Harness Input
Everyone can benefit from feedback, so clarify what works best for you and let others know.

18. Show People You Care
You can never know a person's backstory, so model empathy and humility when addressing performance issues.

19. Make Sure You're Understood

Don't get mad when no one reads your email. Find the best information venues—plural.

20. Give People Feedback They Can Hear

The flip side of accepting feedback is giving it. Begin by clarifying your intentions.

UP NEXT

Now that you've mastered the art of communication, it's time to consider your work habits. How do you get stuff done? Is it working for you? There are lots of ways to approach the day, and we'll cover some typical challenges next.

Part Three

ADAPT YOUR ROUTINES

Supporting the people you work with and being a good communicator take time, and time is a finite resource. You can't get any more of it. It helps to confront some myths and habits you've formed to manage yourself and your work. You're not always aware of your choices until you stop and consider them. These stories and questions help shine a light on the little tweaks and shifts you can make to get where you want to go.

It's not cookie-cutter, so there isn't a best way. It's inspiring to hear how others navigate the realm of getting the best out of themselves, and their insights about personal productivity.

21. Rise, Shine, and Make It Worthwhile
How you start your day impacts the rest of it.

22. Take It In, and Make It Stick
Capturing what you're hearing, watching, or listening to.

23. Let Ink Make You Think
Sharing different approaches to retaining what you read.

24. Form the Habits You Want
The tricks and techniques behind forming and maintaining the habits you want.

25. Define Your Boundaries
Managing remote work and the trend toward being constantly available.

26. Remember a Name and Honor the Person
Becoming good with names is foundational to forming relationships.

21

RISE, SHINE, AND MAKE IT WORTHWHILE

A SENSE OF ACCOMPLISHMENT

A SENSE OF ACCOMPLISHMENT—IT'S A SATISFYING FEELING BECAUSE, AS WE KNOW, THERE'S COMPETITION FOR OUR ATTENTION.

Email is like catnip. Social media scrolling can put you in a trance or take you down a rabbit hole. Choose your platform of poison. There were mornings where hours slipped by and the only thing I'd completed was email. Instituting the Three Ds—Do, Delete, Defer—made me better at it. That set me up to reach "Inbox Zero," but I'd created nothing and time had slipped by. My sense of accomplishment often rang hollow.

Aside from the time slipping by, there's the risk of the multi-tasking swirl. Facing the double-dozen things that need to get done by tackling them simultaneously. Wearing all the hats at once and shooting from the hip left me feeling wired. It's a form of energy, but it's scattershot and exhausting—which calls out for a better approach.

My morning routine has been a work in progress for years (as routines should be). Mark Twain's concept of the "frog" opened up a new framework. His analogy is that eating a live frog is akin to doing the task you most dread. So, if the "frog" is the first thing you take care of in a day, the rest of your work is a cakewalk. Disgusting, but he's got a point. Cue the frog.

Other elements of my routine are a result of a lifetime of interactions and learning:

- Successful people meditate, which led to a 10-minute session courtesy of an app.
- A good friend's grandmother did yoga every morning, and she lived to a spry 103, so a brief routine is just enough most days.
- Gratitude shifts your mindset, so the day begins with three things to be grateful for.
- Surfacing paradoxes provides insight—establishing opposing feelings opens the door for innovation.

- Reflection helps you learn—did you do what you set out to do—what did you take away?

It's a shifting slate, but it builds focus, intention, and a better use of energy throughout the day.

Creativity requires energy, and you may have more juice at the start of a day. Why waste such pristine brain space on administrative tasks? Postpone emails. Do something that deserves your talent. Remember, we're flawed human beings trying to be our best selves and make good choices. Routines help us do that—to be less flawed.

———

THE WISDOM OF THE CROWD

What is your morning routine?

> Mmmmmm ... frogs! I find I'm more nocturnal. I get my best work done at night. But your wisdom still holds true. I try to 'eat frogs' during the day so that I can do more enjoyable creative work at night.
>
> —Ken Eakin, Lean Coach

> My morning ritual includes a walk in nature with the dog. This brings me so much peace and starts my day off on the right foot.
>
> —Kimberly Gray, Station Manager

> Meditation time with my strategic vision board is daily between 7-8 a.m. That time is essential to establish the tone and focus for the balance of my day. Also, I schedule my most enormous frogs on Monday, then

organize all other frogs/complex tasks between 8-11 a.m. Tuesday through Friday.

—Deondra Wardelle, Owner, CEO, and DEIA Coach for On To The Next One Consulting, LLC

REFLECTIONS

It helps to step back and consider how you structure your day. Conjure some peace before you commit to action. If you move your workout to later in the day it could become an energizer to deflect the afternoon slump. If getting to a challenging project is the problem, then it helps to find an accountability partner. If someone is waiting for you, you won't want to let them down. It doesn't matter if you're a night owl or a lark—be cognizant of your energy flow. Respect and exploit it.

INK MAKES YOU THINK

- What is one thing you could experiment with this week to take better advantage of the moments you're at your most creative?
- What might allow you to start your day with a little more presence, intention, or focus?
- What's the theory behind your experiment?

22

TAKE IT IN, AND MAKE IT STICK

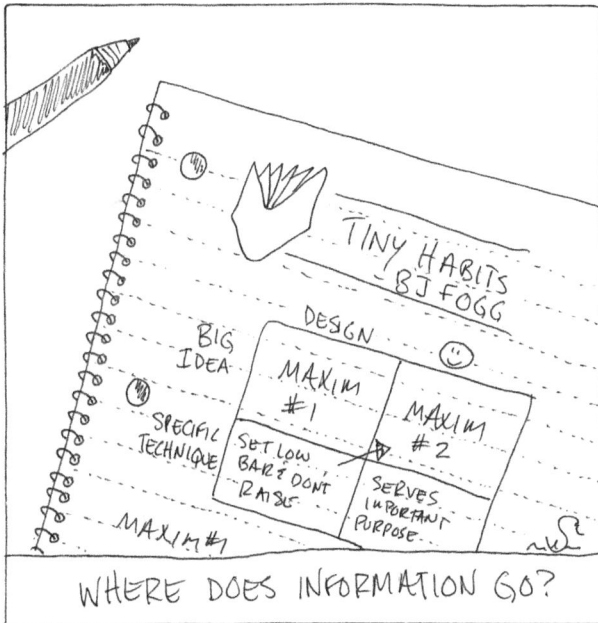

WHERE DOES INFORMATION GO? DO YOU STRESS ABOUT HOW TO CAPTURE IT?

It's easy to get wound up about how to retain what you've learned, what details to write down during phone calls, and where to store information. Being in thrall to my own standards made me freeze until getting it just right.

It took a while to figure out a workable system—or at least the best one for me. In the past it was a struggle to corral scraps of paper into separate topics or place them in chronological order. That note-taking process was by nature *scrappy* and unsatisfying.

The next step was keeping all my notes in spiral-bound notebooks and taking them on the road while traveling for work. Each day started with the date, the city, the client, and whoever else was in the room—"If It's Tuesday, This Must Be Belgium" (for old movie buffs). That helped so much during my road-warrior days it never stopped. Even during the sedentary years of the COVID-19 pandemic, each "home" appeared at the top of the page—as if anyone cared.

Capturing highlights of phone calls along with who's on the call helps me return to questions or salient points during conversations. Writing keeps me listening and paying close attention to what people are saying. Later on, the notebooks provide a reference guide to what we discussed. Cross-referencing the meeting in my digital calendar with my notebook provides an easy lookup system. It's all there— unless my handwriting got all scrawly.

Each completed notebook gets a label with the start-stop dates on the cover. Initially crafting detailed tables of contents for each book became onerous and went by the wayside. There are over sixty books going back as far as 1998. Friends make fun of my massive trove—"As if you'd ever read them!" Oh, but I do.

The current format starts with my morning routines—daily intentions, reflections, and so on. Drawing little icons helps to call out quotes that move me, lightbulbs indicate cool ideas, book icons show-case what to add to my reading list, and little checkboxes signify to-dos. My handwriting is ungainly, sometimes the headings are miss-ing. It will never be perfect—neither will I, so that's fine. It's a constant education. To quote Mark Rosenthal, author of the Lean Thinker blog (which led to a theme in this book), "Ink makes you think."

If you're not capturing what you want, start small—simple is better. Habits stick when they're manageable. An app on your phone, a pocket-sized notepad to capture moments of brilliance, the world is your scrapbook.

―――

THE WISDOM OF THE CROWD

What are your habits for retaining what you want to remember?

> When I'm in person and want to remember things, I pay full attention and listen. I don't take notes as it distracts me from hearing what someone is saying ... and then I don't remember. When I'm reading some-thing, I do my best to try the thing out right away so instead of having 'information,' I turn that into learning and knowledge. If I really want to remember something verbatim, I take a picture of it with my phone.
>
> —Karyn Ross, Activator and Author of *The Kind Leader*

> My RocketBooks! Yes, plural. LOL. They allow me to digitize my notes easily. I can take notes the way I usually do and when I fill up the notebook (about 30/40 pages) I can snap images of what I want to keep and send it to my email or store them in Google Drive. The

notes are searchable, which means I can find specific project notes from six months ago without having to look through six months of notes one by one.

Also the books are reusable and the ink in the Pilot Frixion pens is erasable with water (or the rubberized end on the pens). You can use a single book hundreds of times, saving paper and space on your bookshelf, because only crazy people throw away old notebooks.

—Aisha Cargile, Managing Partner at McCord & Cargile Marketing Resources

I completely agree with 'ink makes you think.' I've also noticed that people respond more positively when they see you taking notes about a problem/opportunity they are presenting.

—Chris Burnham, Host of *The Lean Leadership* podcast

REFLECTIONS

There's more than one way to remember stuff:

- There's writing in old-school, cheap seventy-sheet notebooks, and maybe adding color-coded tape flags for different topics or clients.
- You can use separate notebooks for different realms—Consulting, Sales, Marketing, etc.
- Your cell phones allow you to dictate information to save, or you can capture info in note-type apps where the information is searchable.
- You can take photos of information, people, and events and turn them into albums.

- There are multiple options now for digital notebooks where you're physically writing, but it's uploadable, searchable, and reusable.

INK MAKES YOU THINK

- What is one thing you could try this week to improve your system of capturing information?
- Is it manageable?
- What do you think will happen?

23

LET INK MAKE YOU THINK

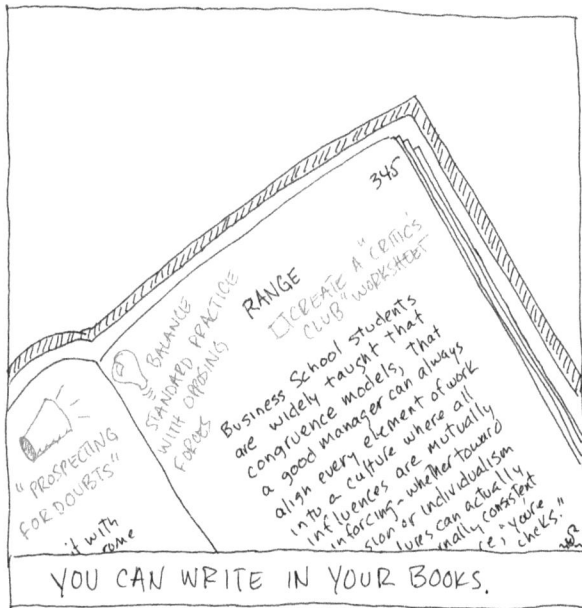

YOU CAN WRITE IN YOUR BOOKS.

YOU CAN WRITE IN YOUR BOOKS.

If you don't already do that, have you ever read a book, but then struggled to remember what you read? Even a great book?

When someone references it you might say, "Oooh, I read that—loved it!" and then find yourself at a loss to remember any specifics. Maybe you highlighted the most moving passages. But you couldn't tell anybody what was in them.

Writing book reviews helped me deal with this—more like mini book reports. They took time, but then I remembered what mattered to me —and the result was a handy personal reference guide. Having a podcast meant interviewing favorite authors and delving deeper into topics that resonated. But book reports take time and, like most people, it feels like a luxury to spend a chunk of it writing about what you've read.

Something along the way transformed my experience. Writing in the books themselves. It didn't initially occur to me to capture my thoughts right there on the page because it seemed somehow wrong. Maybe it's a holdover from checking out library books as a kid, but it felt like defacing something—committing literary vandalism. Having crossed the line, breaking this self-imposed taboo was liberating.

Instead of highlighting or underlining (which is useless for retention), I simply jot down my thoughts. I scrawl out quotes that strike me. I doodle lightbulbs next to ideas sparked by the text. Sometimes I draw a to-do box because the author has spurred me to action. My books are messy and loved. Reading has morphed into an interactive experience (like the one with *Range*, by David Epstein above—a fantastic read).

Some people prefer eBooks, and saving trees is a good argument, reducing the transportation of shipping and all the avoidable production that goes into the printed versions. Yet physical books still hold magic for me. Digital versions allow you to take notes. It's not quite the same, but ...

You are often reading books to become a better-informed human being. You read about concepts, practices, and case studies, so you can apply them to yourself and your community. But how are you going to succeed if you can't remember what was in the book? Research also shows that the act of writing (even more than typing)[1] aids retention. And you can reference your notes whenever you want.

Ink makes you think!

––––––

THE WISDOM OF THE CROWD

How do you remember what you've read?

> I create my own custom index of my notes in the back of the book with page numbers. Now I can pick up any book I have and refer to my custom index to find the important points of what I read.
>
> —Eric Lussier, Principal at NEXT LEVEL Partners®, LLC

> I write and draw in my books, which helps me find important takeaways. What I also do on books that have a lot of good content is create a graphic overview, either on the overall book takeaways or on detailed concepts, as *my* high-level reference for future discussions. They usually create more engaged conversations within our group.
>
> —Jennifer Lacy, Lean Practice Leader at Robins & Morton

> For true retention I tell someone about my favorite passage of the day. Recalling and rephrasing in my own words helps it stick.
>
> —Ashley F. Davis, Paralegal Assistant at Ogletree Deakins

REFLECTIONS

One novel author strategy is allowing the reader to create their own index. And you, dear reader, are the beneficiary of the hand-crafted index. Title your personal index with the categories that are most useful to you. Capture "Quotes," "References," "Books," or whatever appeals. Add topics you want to reference in your own custom section which is a permanent part of your experience.

Of course, you can write or draw in this book. It's the best of all possible worlds.

INK MAKES YOU THINK

- How could you experiment this week to improve how you are retaining what you've read, heard, or learned?
- What resonates?
- Write it down—somewhere.

---

1. https://www.sciencedaily.com/releases/2021/03/210319080820.htm

24

FORM THE HABITS YOU WANT

I DID IT EVERY DAY FOR A WEEK, AND THEN ... NOTHING.

Good or bad, we form habits. What makes me get on the exercise bike? When did I start eating chocolate with my coffee? How do we deal with emails? We're building habits whether we're cognizant or not, so we might as well get better at forming the ones we want. One habit is my morning routine which changes slightly over time. I add new rituals—ones that promise a better day. Some remain, some fade. I took a closer look to understand what makes the difference.

There are some great books out there that address the challenge of starting or kicking habits. *The Power of Habit* by Charles Duhigg lays out a three-part process:

- **Trigger** (something that will kick off the habit)
- **Routine** (the habit)
- **Reward** (something positive that comes of the habit)

If you include these three elements, you can form a habit (or replace one you're done with). Michael Bungay Stanier's *The Coaching Habit* references Duhigg's research to help coaches create a routine of asking better questions. There's other techniques that focus on breaking habits down into smaller activities to make them more manageable.

One habit, formed a few years ago, was to set my intentions for the day. Katie Anderson, author of *Learning to Lead, Leading to Learn*, recommends the approach to keep our actions in alignment with our purpose—who we want to be. I set my intentions and then reflect on how they play out. It's been a few years and that one has become ingrained—it took a moment to tease out why it got a foothold while others didn't. Breaking it down helped.

Inserting "Intentions" into my morning lineup—right after listing three things to be grateful for—gives it prominence. The order works since it reminds me of the larger world around me. Gratefulness is a good segue into considering my intentions and how to approach the day.

At the end of each day, capturing "Actions" makes me list any steps that addressed my intentions. Then it's "Reflections." Any success? Any learnings? What happened? One recent reflection was the downside of being impatient—how it detracts from my being present. Then it hit me—the joy of figuring stuff out is the payoff or Duhigg's "reward." Getting even a little insight feels good. That's the "glue" for this habit.

The habit breaks down into relatively small actions to incorporate— first the intentions, followed by actions, and finally some reflections. It takes less than a minute to document each of these throughout the day. Making a cup of tea takes longer than that. This is a totally manageable habit.

But the rebuke of dusty exercise equipment is evidence for all of us— we don't always succeed.

———

THE WISDOM OF THE CROWD

What do you do to make habits stick?

> When trying to build a new habit, I look for small things to make it easier to follow. To build the habit of working out each morning, I lay out my workout clothes the night before. To build a habit of drinking more water, I set a timer on my phone to go off every 15 minutes (annoying, yes, but incredibly effective!). To build a habit of starting my work day with a review of my calendar, Trello, and email—in that order—I saved those three pages as favorites (in that order) on my bookmarks bar. To work on my habit of healthier

eating, I throw away all of the unhealthy foods I can manage to. If it's easier to follow my new habit, I'm more likely to do it.

—Rebeca Snelling, Author of *Choosing By Advantages: How to Make Sound Decisions* and Leadership Coach at RS Consulting

This reminds me of a great trick I learned from BJ Fogg's book, *Tiny Habits*. For example, I know I'm terrible at drinking water throughout the day. He taught me that instead of setting an output goal, like drinking 64 oz. of water a day, you should set a goal around a tiny habit that will lead to your goal, like filling a glass of water. You become tempted to drink it, then refill it, then drink it ..., ultimately consuming your output for the day. This is more of a process goal to monitor and respond to throughout the day.

—Jennifer Ayers, Executive Director of the Northwest High Performance Enterprise Consortium (NWHPEC)

Perhaps one way to think about intention setting in this way is to identify how the identified actions connect with your purpose or who you want to be. For example, how does daily exercise (an action as a goal) align with who you want to be (a healthy, active person)? Doing this can help connect our goals with our intentions and develop the habits needed to realize the person we want to be and the impact we want to have

—Katie Anderson, Leadership Consultant and Author of *Learning to Lead, Leading to Learn*

REFLECTIONS

Habits can be good or bad ... conscious or unconscious. Some of us struggle to form new habits, and others strive to replace their more insidious rituals. Tracking makes a difference, switching the trigger or prompt to something easy helps, and including some kind of reward helps pave an easier path. Start small, and make it manageable.

INK MAKES YOU THINK

- What is one habit you'd like to form, or reform this week?
- How easy would it be to try out?
- What do you imagine will happen?

25

DEFINE YOUR BOUNDARIES

I'M WORKING AS HARD AS I CAN!

I'M WORKING AS HARD AS I CAN! AND THAT'S NOT ENOUGH.

Do you work late? Weekends? Do people know you are working hard? Is the culture requiring nights and weekends, or is it you?

These questions loomed large while working on a combined project team from two different consulting companies. We had partnered to roll out a continuous improvement transformation for a large multinational corporation. We occupied a classic "war room" at the organization's headquarters.

We spent months together hammering out structure, workshops, and overseas events. There was camaraderie, but there was also competition between the consultants. The unspoken norm was to be the earliest to the office and the last to leave. Looking diligent drove exhaustion. A large portion of those hours were done in a haze of good intentions.

In another organization staff were regularly putting in twelve- and fourteen-hour days. Some new hires resigned as soon as they got the lay of the land, but others were determined to adapt. The job requirements and the harsh culture drove long nights, tough weekends, and inevitable burnout—many left in tears. Turnover was high, but those who stuck it out seemed reluctant to question the demands of their jobs.

With the growing reality of work-from-home arrangements, you can feel obliged to reply to emails the moment they sail into your inboxes. Even if you're not at your computer, you might be a servant to the alerts on your phone, so we're eternally aware if someone wants something from you. The digital tether forms an invisible work leash.

One helpful example comes from a colleague in financial services. As a young intern, she received vital training on a "Model Workweek."

- She checks email and texts three times a day; once in the morning, again after lunch, and then finishes at the end of the day. Otherwise those apps remained silenced.
- She sets expectations with clients and colleagues—call if something's urgent.
- She limits the time she spends on email, and makes sure everything is processed by the end of the day. Those limitations form a deadline for communication.

That structure allows her to get into a flow, and stay productive while being a reliable communicator. She works for herself now, yet never lost those rules of response.

If you're not in a cubicle, or even if you are, what's the best way to be *seen*? If you're *on* all the time, is it the culture? Or is it you? The reality is you're part of the culture. It's often tough to tease out what part you play in the dance of accessibility. But if you don't give it some scrutiny, you fall into the trap of working all the time, and what's the fun in that?

———

THE WISDOM OF THE CROWD

How do you draw limits without disappointing clients, managers, colleagues, or yourself?

> I believe the first step is being self-aware and scheduling the times each day/week that belong to you and no one else. Then identify times that are available for service to others. Once you are clear what your limits are, be upfront about your availability and set realistic expectations.
>
> —Stephanie Hill, Owner of Lightbulb Moment Consulting

Setting and maintaining boundaries is one of the kindest things we can do, for ourselves and others. Small shifts can have a huge impact! For example, When I schedule meetings, they are either 25 minutes or 50 minutes long. This gives me (and others) a small cushion to pause and breathe and not race from one thing to the next.

—Amy Leneker, Leadership Consultant and Certified Dare to Lead™ Facilitator

I decided a long time ago that I need to learn balance, and I've been doing it ever since. Some days I work more and some days less. Some days I don't work at all. But when I'm on vacation, I try not to work at all because that is well-deserved time off. It is more about the quality of work instead of the number of hours you put in.

—Lauren Hisey, Continuous Business Process Improvement Consultant and Speaker

REFLECTIONS

There are different ways to address the advent of "work-from-home" cultures. You can take advantage of the flexibility of being able to work on your own schedules. The downside is when the arrangement leaves people in a no-win situation. Some of you can't help responding to the tug of always being on call, and by doing that you might be failing your families. This is true regardless of whether we're working for ourselves or as part of a larger organization. The trick is to take a hand in this aspect of work culture and declare boundaries for the good of all.

INK MAKES YOU THINK

- What is one method you could try this week to draw a limit with clients, managers, or colleagues?
- What's your new boundary?
- How do you think people will react?

26

REMEMBER A NAME AND HONOR A PERSON

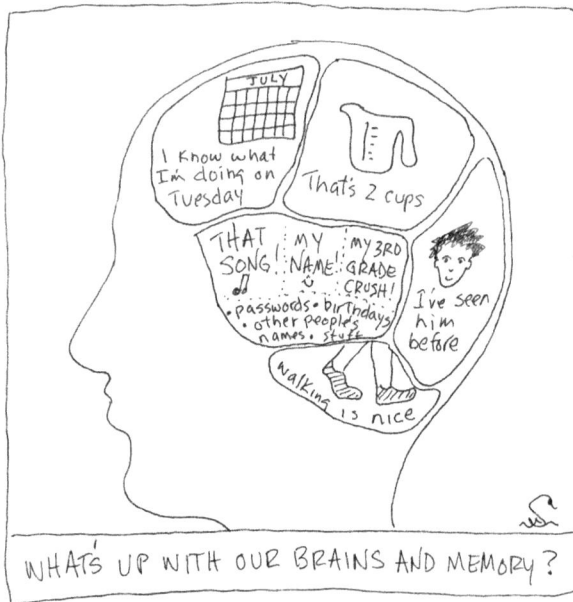

WHAT'S UP WITH OUR BRAINS AND MEMORY?

We seem to have infinite capacity for some stuff—that song you can't get out of your head, what happened on prom night—but more essential things elude us. Do you have trouble remembering people's names?

I learned the hard way decades ago. It was at an offsite, three-day strategy workshop for a mid-sized marine insurance company with over fifty of their leaders. Being new to the consulting team, as well as the client, the event kickoff on the first evening proved pivotal.

We stood in a large circle when my colleague, Ben, instructed everyone to remove their name tags and toss them into the center. Our clients laughed nervously but did as they were told. There was the clicking of plastic hitting the floor as it formed an ungainly pile. Staring at the discarded name tags, I was in absolute horror. I'd never met *any* of these people. I. Knew. No. One.

Ben smiled, approached each person, and addressed them all by name. Their amazement and delight were palpable. It was a cross between awe—how did he do that?—and bewilderment—how do I get through the next three days?

"What's his name?" "Who is she again?" He did his best to keep me connected to the group. My ignorance left me in a panic—ducking out as the situations got sticky. He apologized for not considering how his stunt might leave me at a loss. We remained good friends, mainly because he taught me so many life lessons. This was a big one.

The secret, he said, was that intentions mattered most. You have to *want* to remember a person's name. During an introduction, you hear the other person's name and it's at the forefront of your awareness. Then you say your own name as part of the exchange, and your mind lights up with recognition, "That's me!" The other person's name fades—and then it's gone.

You've got to stay mindful and keep the person's name front and center as soon as you hear it. Then you can use a few other tricks. They might resemble someone you know with the same name, or a famous person. You've also got to repeat their name to yourself until you've got it cold.

Since that day, Ben's "stunt" has been an introductory mainstay of my workshops. It shifts the mood on Day One. Participants' eyes light up as they hear their names, and there's a feeling of connection. Using my nervous morning energy to get to know people makes everything flow.

It may seem like an obvious element, but knowing a person's name is part of building relationships. And forming relationships is a foundational skill for leading others. If you're bad with names that's a reason to get better, not an excuse to avoid it. Make it your intention to learn people's names. You'll form connections that surprise you, and you'll honor those around you.

———

THE WISDOM OF THE CROWD

What memorization techniques do you use?

> I'm sharing a tip that Doug Dunlap gave us many moons ago. He asked us to associate the name with something concrete and imagine an action with that name. Using his name as an example,
>
> Doug: Imagine a Douglas fir tree standing upright.
>
> Action: Imagine that tree jumping up and down on a Dunlop tire!
>
> —Sunitha Narayanan, Leadership Impact Coach

" I'll share a great method I learned from a facilitator to remember the names of class participants: Walk up and have a conversation with each person at their table group as they arrive. Use a piece of paper and write their name in the position they are sitting at the table. Tape it to the end of the table so you can view it during facilitation. After the first hour of class, most of the names come naturally. And ... few people realize you've posted their names.

—Jennifer Ayers, Executive Director of the Northwest High Performance Enterprise Consortium (NWHPEC)

" I struggle with names as well, so I usually start with a list on the wall/whiteboard somewhere with name, role/location, something fun about them or expectations for the workshop. If I go in an order around the room that makes logical sense to me, I can usually recall where people were sitting and enough of their introduction to peek at the list on the wall if I forget. A little visual management, plus as others have said, I tend to remember what I write.

—Shelcy Kamrud, Lean Process Improvement Manager at Mount Sinai Morningside

REFLECTIONS

I shared this one with my husband, who goes into a mild panic when heading into a large gathering. He asks, "Can you remind me who's going to be there? I'm so bad with names." But when he was a young bartender, he knew everyone's drink. Why? Because he wanted to. It mattered to him. His intentions made the difference, and he found a way to remember each person's preferences.

Around that same time, he was rear-ended at an intersection, and when he looked into the rear-view mirror, he saw the driver's face and thought, "Whiskey Sour!" I'm not entirely sure if knowing the driver's drink helped resolve the accident, but the point is there's nothing wrong with his memory. It all starts with intention.

INK MAKES YOU THINK

- What other ways can you think of to try remembering something?
- What is something that you have been effective at remembering?
- How could this past experience help you with something you find more challenging?

ADAPT YOUR ROUTINES—LOOKING BACK

Part Three

Part of having an impact in this world is how you show up. There's a lot that goes into that. How you start your day impacts you and the people you're working with. Remembering what you're reading determines the wisdom you can impart to others. If you're about to head to a gathering, how are you going to remember people's names? Are you drawing lines around when you're available so you can be present when it matters? Maybe you decided to let your ideas percolate for a bit. If you did test out some new behaviors, what did you discover?

Reflect on the impact of your decisions. Consider the shift in your mindset. Writing things down affects the way you think. The way you think impacts the way you behave. And of course, once you change your behavior, you see the fruits of your actions.

Did you add anything to the index at the back of this book? You can inspire yourself simply by reading your own words. What are you planning to try?

KEY POINTS SUMMARY

21. Rise, Shine, and Make It Worthwhile
Start your day with the most important or challenging things you need to accomplish. Don't waste your morning on administrative tasks if that's your most creative stretch.

22. Take It In, and Make It Stick
Use your journal, or however you capture information, the way it helps you most—there's no "right" way.

23. Let Ink Make You Think
Books are meant to serve you—write in them if you want!

24. Form the Habits You Want
You've got routines whether you formed them consciously or not—might as well pay attention and form the ones you truly want.

25. Define Your Boundaries
Draw limits with people—or you'll drown in other people's expectations.

26. Remember a Name and Honor the Person
Most people are bad at names. It takes intention to be good, and you have to know a person's name to form a relationship.

UP NEXT

Now that you've adjusted your routines, it's time to put them to higher use—creativity. What's your process? How do you approach making stuff? How do you craft texts, emails, memos, presentations, training, white papers, standard operating procedures, and other forms of content? All of these require imagination, which comes next.

Part Four

EXPAND YOUR REACH

You may not consider yourself *creative* but that doesn't stop you from creating. Every time you pose yourself a question, put pen to paper, or fingers to keyboard, you are drawing on your imagination. You might tap your own experience, collaborate with a colleague, or conduct research to find out how others have approached the challenge at hand. The barriers to finding information may have fallen away with the internet, but the sheer abundance of facts and resources can lead to brain freeze.

When do you tap your creative process and what's the best approach? Simply becoming conscious of what works best is a first step. Then you can experiment with attractive adaptations. Like it or not, you're a creator. Begin!

27. Set Your Brain Up for Success
Take advantage of how your brain is wired.

28. Bring It On, and Get It Out There
You're a creator, so how do you go from idea-to-reality?

29. Don't Let Perfect Be the Enemy of Good
Reduce the pressure of perfection.

30. Ignore Your Inner Naysayers
How to keep from editing yourself unnecessarily.

31. Use Your Own Voice
How to detect and deflect your own camouflage.

32. Give the Gift of Clarity
Simplify so others comprehend, and care.

33. Free Your Beginner's Mind
Embrace the boldness of your younger self.

27

SET YOUR BRAIN UP FOR SUCCESS

WHERE DO YOU GET YOUR BEST IDEAS?

Do you struggle when brainstorming in groups? Are there extended periods of "crickets" where waiting out the silence doesn't work? Is the resulting list of ideas less-than-inspired?

When trying to come up with improvement ideas, I used to teach ideation techniques to help my clients flex their creative muscles. We played with methods like "Anti-Solution" by brainstorming the opposite of the goal. The results were hilariously close to reality, which made it an effective ice breaker. We tried "Analogy" by diverting our solutions to a different arena. The results were better than straight brainstorming, but later conversations revealed that no one was using the tools outside of class. This was discouraging.

Group brainstorming over video introduces a new set of challenges. Remote work denies us the in-person sparks, yet the problem isn't simply the venue—it's the process. We're not taking advantage of how our brains work. The key to enhanced idea flow lies in our neural network. A big window into that reality came from an early mentor.

My colleague Mitch Ditkoff, the author of *Storytelling at Work,* uses an enlightening question to spark group innovation, "Where do you get your best ideas?" The results rarely vary: walking the dog, taking a shower, knitting, etc. No one ever says, "At my desk" or "In a conference room at work." Having incorporated Mitch's technique for over thirty years helps confirm a universal truth about brainstorming— the group does best on its own. Still, there are ways to use our individual reality to help the group.

A bit of neuroscience[1] digging revealed that solitary, rote activity— like washing dishes or working out—conjures theta brain waves. Theta waves—unlike the beta waves of group brainstorming— promote peak idea flow. The moments between waking and sleeping do it too. Office settings aren't ideal, so how do you take advantage of these theta waves?

My personal go-to when stuck, is a bike ride. The pedals are spinning, and my brain is free to entertain solutions. When coaching groups, they first have to clarify a "How can we … ?" question—the innovation challenge they are facing. Then everyone gets "Theta Time" to conjure idea flow. They can meet remotely or in person once they've had a chance to think. The resulting session becomes a richer convergence of ideas. There are benefits from dual-purpose dog walking, and it's much more gratifying. It takes a little longer, but there are far fewer "crickets" and the ideas are superior.

———

THE WISDOM OF THE CROWD

What helps you get the best ideas from yourself and others?

> When possible, take a brainstorming walk together as a team. Pair up, talk about the problem being solved, the insights, opportunities, and start working through it. Rotate the pairs as the walk continues and share responsibility to record or take notes during the walk.
>
> —Jared Akins, Business Transformation Leader at Avista

> I always encourage my teams to reflect at the end of the day and before the session starts, during 'down time.' I believe the mind relaxes and opens to new possibilities that way.
>
> —Adam Lawrence, Author of *The Wheel of Sustainability*

> When I facilitate a meeting, I try to make it span over an afternoon between Day One and the next morning. I design the agenda to brainstorm at the end of Day One

and the beginning of Day Two. This gives the participants a chance to discuss ideas at dinner and then get
some solo time (gym, shower, getting ready for bed, etc.)
to think. The ideas on Day Two are much deeper,
richer, and well-thought-out, and usually become
action items.

—John Dyer, President of JD&A, Inc. - Process Innovations and Author of *The Façade of Excellence*

REFLECTIONS

In terms of where you get your best ideas, if you favor the moments
between waking and sleeping, it's best to keep a notepad handy on
the night table. If you find your creativity fares best during rote activities, try capturing notes with a cell phone or recording voice memos
as ideas pop into existence. The idea of walking in pairs recalls Aristotle's Lyceum, which was a peripatetic philosophy school. It basically translates to "walking" school. If it was good enough for
Aristotle …

INK MAKES YOU THINK

- How do you help yourself or others get their best ideas?
- What's a recent example of a time when you came up with
  something worthwhile?
- What's one experiment you could try the next time you need
  to come up with solutions?

---

1. https://www.scientificamerican.com/article/what-is-the-function-of-t-1997-12-22/

28

BRING IT ON, AND GET IT OUT THERE

DO YOU KNOW YOUR CREATIVE PROCESS?

DO YOU KNOW YOUR CREATIVE PROCESS?

Do you consider yourself a creator? You are, and it's worth considering how you go about it. The more aware you are, the easier it is to take your "genius" idea to the next level. Most lightbulb moments dim with disuse. What gets you from that initial spark to a home run?

"Genius is one percent inspiration, ninety-nine percent perspiration." Although often attributed to Thomas Edison, this quote stems from the work of the academic Kate Sanborn. Her point was that genius requires more heavy lifting than spark. It takes effort to bring thoughts to fruition.

A colleague recently asked me what my creative process was, which got me curious. Take a look, and think about yours. You have one, whether you are aware of it or not.

- **Capture:** Ideas come at odd moments, so a method of capture is key. There's a notepad on my nightstand for the midnight "aha." During the day, there's a spiral notebook. Ideas get an image of a lightbulb. I put them at the top of the page, so it's easy to flip through and find them.
- **Set a Limit:** Next, establish a deadline. Self-enforcement is tough, so including someone else in the process keeps me honest. That's only one of the reasons to involve others. We'll get to that.
- **Find the Juice:** Time of day is critical for me. Earlier is better than later since creativity requires energy—no wasting entire mornings on email. Maintaining gusto is a worthy quest.
- **Cut Loose:** Put pen to paper. They don't have to be the *best* words—but there has to be something to work with. More on that later.
- **Percolate:** This step requires the theta brain waves referenced in Chapter 27. When hitting this stage I engage in rote activities like washing the dishes or mining the

moments between waking and sleeping. Research shows they conjure the best idea flow. So, fold the laundry, take a walk, or sleep on it!

- **Collaborate:** Improv training leads to "yes, and ..." Time to consider connecting with a colleague. Are there other approaches floating around in the ether? Are there ways to incorporate the ideas that appeal? Swapping concepts with others is always a good thing.
- **Polish:** Time to get picky. Touch it up and pare it down. There's a macabre saying (with disputed origins) that helps during this phase, "Kill your darlings." I might have a nice turn of phrase, an entertaining nugget, but does it fit? Does it need to go *here*? If not, let it go.
- **Ship:** Meaning finish the job and get it out there. Finally, pragmatism and courage. I don't let "perfect" be the enemy of good. I do it scared, hit "send," and move on to the next one.

Remember, you *do* create, even if it's emails, spreadsheets, and meals. You do it already. Recognize that you are already creating every day. You don't need to "become" creative. You are creating. And once you consider your process, you can get better.

Setting time limits and staying detached from the outcome helps with the final stage of the creative process. To "ship" means to finish the job and get it out into the world. And you don't have to do it alone —things get interesting when you include others. Do it tactically so the deadline feels real, but also because it's good practice to bump up against the brains of others.

———

THE WISDOM OF THE CROWD

What makes your creative process tick?

> For me, it comes at odd times throughout the day. As soon as I get a thought, I either write it down or send myself an email. Once or twice a month, I take those ideas and brainstorm some more. Then I will develop a plan.
>
> —Lauren Hisey, Continuous Business Process Improvement Consultant and Speaker

> Recently my creative process is fueled by how useful I perceive my 'genius idea' to be for the people who will benefit. If I see a clear need and a group of interested people who can also see themselves benefitting from it, I am motivated to persevere. This is, however, a brand-new discipline for me that has come from recent experiences. I am very determined to practice the tenets of the book *Essentialism* by Greg McKeown. So, my values of community and collaboration drive my decision to stick with it, shelve it for now, come back to it later, or maybe never!
>
> —Néha Singh, CEO of PACE.global

> Often collaboration takes my ideas, marries them with the ideas of others, and creates something that I never envisioned. When I limit my ideas to just my 'bubble' they often don't grow to where they need to be.
>
> —Dwayne Butcher, Digital Transformation and Continuous Improvement Expert

REFLECTIONS

Once you acknowledge your own creative process, you'll find that it's personal yet communal. Don't neglect to "get amongst it." Talk to people, observe, and reflect. Be mindful of the trap of becoming an idea person. There's an Irish proverb to this point, "You'll never plough a field by turning it over in your mind." Get into the field.

INK MAKES YOU THINK

- Have you ever considered your own creative process?
- What are the things you might do unconsciously?
- Once you know what works, how might you take advantage of your best practices?

29

DON'T LET PERFECT BE THE ENEMY OF GOOD

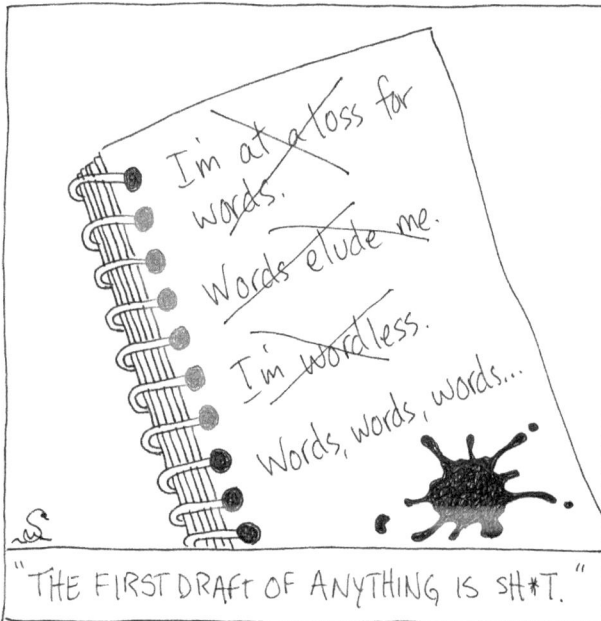

"THE FIRST DRAFT OF ANYTHING IS SH*T."

Hearing this made me laugh. It also made me realize how much pressure I used to put on myself to craft each individual sentence to perfection. My focus could be so intense that I'd lose the plot on the larger piece. It was a case of not seeing the forest for the trees. The big picture was at the mercy of adjectives.

Have you ever stared at the space where the first paragraph should be —just willing it to exist? Have you labored over selecting the exact right word until the words stop making sense? Do you waste time wishing you wrote as well as [fill in the blank]? Have you ever placed so much pressure on a sentence that you began to resent your keyboard? You are not alone.

This quote is attributed to Hemingway and it's liberating. He may be alluding to the hard work of writing but there's a whiff of, "You're not that great. Get over yourself and simply start writing." If Hemingway's first drafts weren't perfect, then why should yours be? This applies regardless of what you're writing; an email, a presentation, an executive summary, a social media post, a limerick, or a text. Give yourself license to cut loose and create. It's liberating to take yourself down a peg. Expect less of your first efforts and see what happens.

Will you have to edit it? Guaranteed. Will the second draft be great? Maybe. Maybe you'll need to tighten it up some more. You may end up tossing it out altogether and starting fresh. The key is to begin with the assumption that whatever you're creating is not going to be perfect—it's planned imperfection.

Are you still struggling with how to begin? There's nothing magic about starting with the first sentence. What if you're more interested in the second paragraph? What if you've got a great ending in mind? Start there. Go where the spirit moves you. Once you start hitting the keyboard with abandon, you'll create your own momentum. The words will appear, and you'll have something to work with. Editing is easier than getting the first draft down. Editing is *much* easier when you've got words to edit.

And you can apply that to more than writing. Want to experiment with something new? A different direction? An alternative technique? Just start. You can change your tack, see how it works, and refine your approach. You can advance or retreat from any position you take. There may be writing involved, or the "draft" may be visual. You might want to try out a physical set up. It's all possible if you simply get rolling.

———

THE WISDOM OF THE CROWD

How do you approach that first draft?

> Equally dangerous is getting stuck in the editing perfection loop. The second draft is sh*t, as is the third, and fourth. This has to be balanced with the Steve Jobs quote: 'artists ship'.
>
> —Jamie Flinchbaugh, Author of *People Solve Problems*

> Without the burden of perfection, all things are possible.
>
> —Brian Buck, Boldness Coach, Business Consultant, and Keynote Speaker

Voltaire wrote, "The perfect is the enemy of good." I know this to be true because I see it every morning in the mirror. I also see it in several executive coaching clients. These well-educated, smart people suffer anxiety, lack of self-confidence, and Imposter Syndrome due to perfectionism. My coaching advice is to practice daily self-talk where they address themselves as "good enough." To shed the weight of being a perfectionist, and consider themselves on a lifelong journey of continuous improvement. They—and everyone else— are 'works in progress.'

—Thomas Schlick, Operational Consultant, Executive Coach, Adjunct Professor, and Author of *Jumpstart Your Service Revolution*

REFLECTIONS

You may feel the need to *get it right*. But that sense of pressure doesn't make the process go faster or result in something better. What helps is the freedom to produce sh*t. Even if you can't help yourself and end up working harder to get that first draft right, you still end up needing a second draft. You make the road by walking. Putting pen to paper is what matters.

INK MAKES YOU THINK

- Do you have a project due?
- Are you helping others who have to pull something together?
- How will you give yourself and others the freedom to produce, knowing the first draft is imperfect?
- What do you think will happen?

The second draft is imperfect too, so start!

30

IGNORE YOUR INNER NAYSAYERS

STOP THE CHATTERING MONKEYS.

Do you get waylaid (or hijacked) by the discouraging voices in your head? Are they what keep you from being bold?

The chattering monkeys come from an early mentor of mine, Bennet Neiman, who wrote *Slay the Dragons, Free the Genie* (and taught me to remember names the hard way: see Chapter 27). He made me realize that we edit ourselves far more than others might.

How many times have you been in a meeting with an idea but held back only to hear a colleague contribute the same idea? How often have you wanted to try something new but convinced yourself it wasn't worth trying? Or maybe you suspected it *was* worthy, but your inner dialogue convinced you the odds of success were insurmountable.

You are in your own head for most of the day and you may have learned over time to be cautious. Yet your 5-year-old self would try anything. As you age you get better at silently listing all the risks and doubts. You can "awfulize" at an alarming rate.

We talk at about 125 words per minute, and we can process words at about 800 words per minute[1]. According to Ethan Cross[2], author of *Chatter*, your "inner" speed of processing is 4,000 words per minute. It would be hard for anyone to withstand the rapid-fire descent down a rabbit hole. If you don't stem the tide, you can talk yourself out of just about anything.

When experiencing a spate of "can't do" self-talk, there are a few remedies that make a difference for me. One is a quote from Henry Ford, "Whether you think you can or think you can't, you're right." That's a reminder that the chattering monkeys are your personal inventions. Own them.

They exist to keep you safe from harm, ridicule, or loss. They are great defenders of the status quo, so they also hold you back from your own brilliance. The first step is to recognize their role and climb back out of the rabbit hole. The next step is to use some of your own instincts. What would you say to help someone else move toward action? Use your techniques on yourself.

Another great thing to do is to switch into a physical activity. Remember what you learned in Chapter 27—Set Your Brain Up for Success. You can conjure the peak idea flow of theta brain waves when you take a walk or wash the dishes. A walk in nature can provide as much stimulant as a cup of coffee. Relax, there's no need to give up coffee. The bonus of a quick stroll includes both a jolt of energy and a boost to your thinking patterns. Maybe leave your voice memo on while you're out ...

You can also phone a friend. You know who's on your short list. Reach out and ask for perspective. It doesn't have to take much time, but the simple act of having a conversation slows your processing rate way down. It's tougher for the monkeys to interrupt. It also helps to laugh. What cracks you up? Jokes work because they surprise you with a shift in perspective. Sometimes, that's all you need.

———

THE WISDOM OF THE CROWD

What's your favorite technique to circumvent the chattering monkeys?

> When my inner voice says I'm not going to be successful, or it tells me, "You shouldn't do this because you aren't good at it," and I listen to that inner critic, I always end up making bad choices. It's funny because when I look back on my life, the times when I said, "Nope, I am doing it" or "I got this" to the inner critic, they've turned out to be the best decisions.

So now, I remind myself of all the times that I didn't listen to the naysayers and I was successful. My best advice is to list all the times you did it despite the fear and were successful. Then remind yourself, if you did it once, you can do it again; trust yourself.

—M. Genevieve Pawlak, President & Chief Alchemist of Prime Alchemy

I stop and put together a jigsaw puzzle on one of my apps.

—Dr. Cindy Young, TEDx Speaker, Knowledge Management Expert

My favorite way out of this is to either walk it off, or, when the weather is bad, put on loud music and dance it off.

—Gemma Jones, Improvement Coach, Founder of SPARK Improvement Ltd.

REFLECTIONS

What helps is a physical *go-to* activity to short-circuit the negative self-talk. That's something within your control. You may also want to list your own coaching questions that help interrupt the chatter. Have them on hand when the fog is obstructing your view of the big picture. Whatever helps stifle your inner naysayers, or at least turn the volume down.

Ink Makes You Think

- What's one thing you're game to try the next time your inner dialogue fails to help you?
- When you start to doubt your own ideas, how will you give your genius a fighting chance?

- What do you think might happen?

  _____

1. https://www.speakeasyinc.com/hearing-vs-listening/#:~:text=The%20average%20rate%20of%20speech,about%20800%20words%20per%20minute.
2. Ethan Cross, *Chatter: The Voice in Our Head, Why it Matters* (Crown, 2021)

31

USE YOUR OWN VOICE

CORPORATE CAMOUFLAGE vs. AUTHENTICITY

CORPORATE CAMOUFLAGE VS. AUTHENTICITY, AND THE CORPORATION OFTEN WINS.

It's often mechanical so it can be a surprise to discover it in your own communication efforts.

My revelations stem from working with my colleague Tracy. We read each other's work. My job as editor is to strip out every "really," "very," "surely," and other "extra" words from existence—joyously, I might add. Exclamation marks and redundancies rarely survive. The writing is always better, but that's not all that matters.

In contrast, she reads my work and says things like, "I know you're invested in this idea, but I don't hear *you*." Or "I know you feel strongly about this but I'm not sensing it here." She says it with care, but it always stings a bit. And she's right. Your writing style shouldn't replicate your speaking style, but readers should still be able to hear your voice. And that means both how you think and how you feel. Your speaking style should represent who you are.

The business world traditionally trains us to remove emotion from our communications—written and spoken. Neither white papers nor team meetings should include tirades. Fair enough. But what's left? Facts and data, and they often fail to move people. You may be trying to convince people to do something worthwhile. You might be offering advice or suggesting a method that could change their lives for the better. What you *want* is for people to act, while using language that fails to inspire. It's a common disconnect.

We often adopt official personas—public-sanctioned versions of ourselves. You might not feel secure in your position, or you may sense the workplace demands it. But is that who people want to hear? There are times in your career that call for caution, and that should evolve as you mature. It shouldn't stay the norm.

My colleague Deondra often stops me in my tracks with vivid turns of phrase like, "Just put the skunk on the porch." Anyone listening knows it's time to stop avoiding the unspoken "skunk" of an issue at hand. Her colorful, idiosyncratic expressions upend conversations with the mirth of truth. Yet she was rarely expressing herself the same way in group settings. When I called her on it, she admitted she'd been saving her gems for her inner circle. No more—the world was missing out.

Do you do this as well? Do you edit who you present to the world? Is it out of necessity or habit? What about those you work with? Do you hear their true voices? Are they bringing their whole selves to their work? Give them permission to put their voices into their efforts. Making a difference—moving people to change—requires passion and authenticity at all levels.

THE WISDOM OF THE CROWD

How do you remain authentic?

> I have an accountability partner I trust implicitly, regardless of what her feedback is.
>
> —Lynn McLaughlin, Author and Host of the podcast, *Taking the Helm*

> I am proud to report that I'm leaning in to sharing the 'most captivating version of myself.'
>
> —Deondra Wardelle, Owner, CEO, and DEIA Coach for On To The Next One Consulting, LLC

> One thing that a Lean consultant told me years ago when I was an employee was, 'Dorsey, you have to bring *yourself* to this work.' That was so enlightening and empowering. I kind of thought I had to be someone else—someone with all the answers, who knew what to

do. Her comment gave me the freedom to bring *my* strengths to Lean—which included not just analysis but also kindness and humor. I've never forgotten that comment and try to still remember. Be yourself.

—Dorsey Sherman, MHSA, ACC, and President of Modèle Consulting

REFLECTIONS

It might reflect a certain level of privilege to be able to bring your authentic self to the workplace. Some feel the need to temper how much of their own voice it's okay to share especially when starting out. It may take until midcareer, but embracing your voice can be transformational. There's power, freedom, and a greater reach when you speak for yourself. Consider how much energy it takes *not* to be yourself.

INK MAKES YOU THINK

- Do you bring yourself to work?
- What's one place and one way you could let you be you?
- Do you have an accountability partner to help you find your voice?
- If you don't have one, who might be good for that role?

32

GIVE THE GIFT OF CLARITY

MARK TWAIN ONCE SAID, "I APOLOGIZE FOR SUCH A LONG LETTER—I DIDN'T HAVE TIME TO WRITE A SHORT ONE."

This is one of those paradoxes we know to be true. It's easy to dash off our thoughts, yet it takes time to distill them into something coherent. How many times have you gotten an email that took a few reads to understand? Sometimes you slog to the third paragraph to find the point.

A friend of mine used to leave long messages on my answering machine. This was before smartphones and digital voicemail. This is back when there was a machine capturing voices on tiny tape cassettes. She often left such lengthy messages she completely used up the tape. During consulting road trips, that meant there was no way for anyone else to leave a message. She meandered quite a bit, as if she were deciding why she'd called while she was talking. She was a little insulted when I asked if she could maybe decide on her message before she called me. But I've been just as guilty.

A busy client used to respond, "A-B-C it for me" when receiving my emails. Terse, but it helped train me to organize my thoughts and form outlines of discussions or summarize next steps. Another annoying acronym is TL;DR which translates to "Too Long; Didn't Read." Using cryptic shorthand makes this one feel a bit tit-for-tat. It has a vague subtext that since you've wasted someone's time with a long missive, they're going to stick you with an acronym you might need to look up.

Those are less-than-welcome responses, yet they get at an issue worth examining. If you don't take the time to clarify what you're saying, then the burden falls to the person on the receiving end. Some information genuinely requires detail, and you should include what's needed. Most of the time you're too busy to review what you've written, so you hit send and shift the burden to the reader.

You may also be in position to help others tighten their message. You might be parsing paragraphs to discover a question or a point. Paraphrasing Richard Sheridan, author of *Chief Joy Officer*, "It's a pile of manure, but there's a pony in there somewhere." When searching for said "pony," you could guide those you work with to revisit their text and clarify what they're trying to say.

Not all texts require this attention, and Mark Twain and Hemingway form an interesting team here. Hemingway advises us to simply write with abandon, and Twain points out that we're not excused from crafting the second draft. There's creativity at any level of writing and producing.

By taking the onus on yourself to reflect on what you've written and tighten up what you're saying, you raise the level of your work. Unless you're specifically asking for edits—sending people the "sh*tty" first draft leads to confusion and wastes time. You can do better. Your readers appreciate the effort and it gives you a better chance at getting what you're after.

———

THE WISDOM OF THE CROWD

What writing habits have you developed to tighten your prose before you hit "send"?

> My tightening writing habits: brain dump in bullet points, prioritize and clarify, remove unnecessary points, and draw a picture or take a photo if I can't explain it concisely.
>
> —Chandra Boersma, Lean Coach at Statistics Canada

> I use the built-in grammar checker in the word processing software to identify passive voice. Cutting out the passive voice always shortens the text. Instead of composing a LinkedIn post, write a Tweet. It's amazing

what the constraint of 280 characters can do for your writing.

—Bella Englebach, Author of *Creatively Lean*

Around fifteen years back, my boss at the time gave me a copy of the Kim Long book, *Writing in Bullets*. It helped.

—Stewart Bellamy, Lean Trainer and Coach

REFLECTIONS

There are lots of interesting techniques like using bullet points, removing *fancy* words or, for more important texts, reciting each sentence out loud. You also need to rethink the idea that longer texts and lengthy words are a sign of intelligence. True brilliance is being able to explain the complex with simplicity.

INK MAKES YOU THINK

- Are you guilty of dashing off "treatises" instead of notes?
- What's one technique you're game to try when crafting your next email?
- How might people respond?

Write it down. Now shorten it.

33

FREE YOUR BEGINNER'S MIND

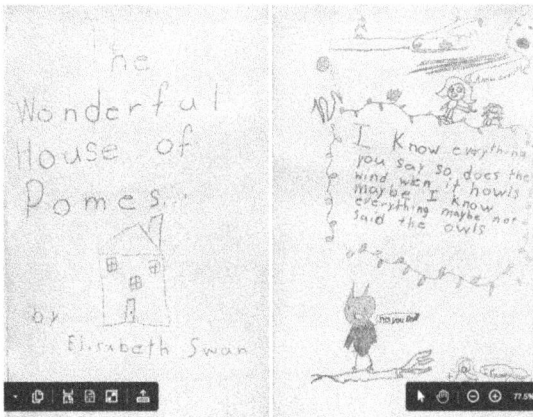

TIME TO THINK LIKE A KID ?

SOMETIMES YOU NEED TO THINK LIKE A KID.

What did you dare to do at age 10, but wouldn't consider now?

I wrote, illustrated, and published a book of poetry at that age. My father used his office mimeograph machine (precursor to the photo-copier) to produce the four-page, block-buster-to-be, which accounts for the faded color in the sample pages. The misspellings, drooping lines, and wandering margins make clear he had zero editorial input. His daughter was the chief architect of this gem.

My father supplied me with construction paper and cardboard to create a book display. He suggested selling my new book and offered to drive me to town to make it happen. That sounded like the logical next step. Authors write books for others to read, so naturally there were people who would want to buy my book.

He helped me bring a fresh stack of my slim volume in a self-deco-rated (construction-paper polka dots on cardboard) box to the local bookshop. The owners were friends of my parents and seemed happy to put my masterpiece on the counter for twenty-five cents a pop. I was giddy with pride.

Now part of a book-writing club, and a few years older, we discuss strategies, trade resources, and encourage each other to write. We discuss style guides, publishing options, and we interview published authors for tips on the book process. We're all capable writers, and yet a common question about our own work is, "Would anyone want to read this?" Not surprisingly, we all share the same doubts.

But my 10-year-old self doubted nothing! She happily showed her book to strangers. She trotted it out to perform readings for guests. She regularly begged to be driven to the bookstore to see if she'd made another quarter. Big money!

Unearthing this faded treasure made me want to honor such audacity in myself and others. Maturity and experience make us better at what we do. Yet for some reason, that same process can leave us less inclined to share our gifts. The confidence and bravery of our younger selves is worth tapping.

There will always be moments when you are challenged to see yourself as capable. There may be promising options you're not considering that you should. Jobs or potential promotions you don't pursue that you could. People you could inspire with your boldness who are waiting for you.

Sometimes you need to think like a kid.

_____

THE WISDOM OF THE CROWD

What do you do to channel your brazen, 10-year-old spirit?

> The 'beginner's mind' is important to both courage and problem solving. One of the many interesting commonalities between Lean and Zen.
>
> —Kevin Meyer, Co-Founder of Gemba Academy

> The judge in our own head comes from somewhere. From someone or from many 'someones' who judge us and our ideas. We take that on and learn to judge ourselves and be unkind to ourselves. It stems from being judged and treated unkindly by others. Be kind to others so they can learn how to be kind to themselves!
>
> —Karyn Ross, Activator and Author of *The Kind Leader*

> I once experienced these three Senseis (Lean coaches) who continuously admonished our team to 'think like a 12-year-old.' At first it seemed weird to me, this was a business process, and I did not understand what they meant. As the days passed it became more obvious.

They told us to think back to when we were 12. We could accomplish almost anything we set our minds to, before we became more jaded as adults, 'knowing things won't work because ...' Since then, this phrase has stuck with me and I use it to refresh myself when tackling new projects.

—Dan McDonnell, Principal at Gemba Coach, LLC

REFLECTIONS

As you reflect on the bravery of your youth, you may have no memory of the results. But it's always a happy reflection. It's a good reminder, when drawing on that courage, to consider the journey as part of the accomplishment. The key is to take action. To quote Johann Wolfgang von Goethe, "Whatever you can do or dream you can, begin it. Boldness has genius, power, and magic in it." Genius, power, and magic are nothing to sneeze at.

INK MAKES YOU THINK

- What challenge have you backed down from recently?
- What have you dismissed as a possibility for yourself?
- What's one thing you might try?
- What do you think will happen?

Now channel your heedless 10-year-old self.

EXPAND YOUR REACH—LOOKING BACK

Part Four

You might not even consider yourself to be creative, let alone allow yourself the time to reflect on, or improve, your creative process. When you tap your mind, how do you capture ideas, how do you judge your ideas? The trick is to remain conscious of your approach to invention and the gifts you bring. It's also on you to challenge others to do the same. It's often easier to help others see and realize what they're capable of. Consider how you dare others to embrace their own creativity, and use that same message on yourself.

Reflect on your own stories and see how your path to genius can change.

KEY POINTS SUMMARY

27. Set Your Brain Up for Success
The workplace, or structured work, might not be where you do your best thinking.

28. Bring It On, and Get It Out There
Recognize that you do create, as a first step—now you can get better at it.

29. Don't Let Perfect Be the Enemy of Good
You're unlikely to craft brilliance out of the gate—use that knowledge to free yourself.

30. Ignore Your Inner Naysayers
You are generally your own worst critic—so find a way to shrug off your inner judge.

31. Use Your Own Voice
If you've been trained to adopt a corporate persona, reconsider whether it still serves you.

32. Give the Gift of Clarity
If there's no word limit, it's up to you to pare your messages down for clarity.

33. Free Your Beginner's Mind
When opportunity strikes, view it through your 10-year-old eyes and leap.

UP NEXT

Creativity doesn't have to be a solo process. You are often at your best when you collaborate and build with others. This means you need to be mindful of how you approach those around you. Your attitude and behavior can make the difference between innovative co-creation and stalled efforts. More on that next.

Part Five

TREAT PEOPLE WITH RESPECT

Part of your journey may be to gain mastery over a chosen field. Whatever your pursuit, there's a critical parallel quest to get better at interacting with others. You're busy, you've got pressures and responsibilities to carry out. You may be inclined to see those as separate from how you deal with others, but they are inextricably intertwined. How you treat people impacts their interest in following you. As Maya Angelou said, "People will forget what you said, people will forget what you did, but people will never forget how you made them feel."

You're modeling leadership at every turn—is it a model worth emulating? Before you consider the impact of your thinking and behavior on yourself, look at how those things make a difference in the lives of others.

34. Be Generous in Your Praise
Acknowledging people is easy, and makes all the difference.

35. Help Others Navigate the Unknown
Learning is uncomfortable, so help people through the messy middle.

36. Give New Leaders a Fighting Chance
How often are people promoted without any leadership training?

37. Go from Setback to Insight
How to help yourself and others move past missed expectations.

38. Lay a Path for Others
What happens when you remove yourself from the equation?

39. Be a Leader People Want to Follow
Remember to look behind you.

40. Unite Your Tribes
Organizational success requires connection.

41. Create the Ties that Bind You to Community
How do you build and maintain your network?

34

BE GENEROUS IN YOUR PRAISE

GIVE PEOPLE CREDIT—IT'S FREE! YET SOMEHOW, DESPITE THE RELATIVE BARGAIN, THERE IS A SCARCITY OF PRAISE.

"Why should I encourage my workers? No one ever encouraged me."

This is a quote from an incredibly accomplished female colleague who started her own design firm. She succeeded in an overwhelmingly male-dominated field. She wrote books, won worldwide contracts, and built her own celebrated organization.

The comment shocked me.

When pressed, she said having to struggle without praise made her tougher. Others took credit for her work throughout her career, and she wanted the women in her firm to grow thicker skins. She didn't want them expecting praise. She wanted them to become immune to criticism. You are defined by your struggles, it's true. But should you withhold praise, credit, or encouragement?

There are lots of reasons *not* to give people credit for their work—you're too busy, you're unaware of their efforts, or you figure a paycheck is affirmation enough. You might have a misdirected sense of stoicism. Maybe, like my colleague, no one ever recognized your efforts so you never developed the habit of recognizing others. It could be a backlash against the perceived "everyone-deserves-a-trophy" syndrome. Whatever the cause, depriving people of affirmation seems a miserly way to go through life.

This is especially true, since the easiest way to get along in this world is to get in the habit of acknowledging the efforts of others. Habit is the pivotal word here. If you make it a *habit* to give people credit, that sets some pretty cool things in motion. Being credited makes people feel seen, appreciated, and respected. As Daniel Pink[1] showcased in his book *Drive*, acknowledgement is often a more powerful motivator than money. Motivated people do great things. One of those things might be to give credit to others—it's like compounding interest, only human.

And it's free. Praise is not a luxury. It costs you nothing to say, "nice work!" It simply means paying attention. You are impacted by so many—often in ways you're not always aware of. The more you acknowledge others—the more people rise in response. This could get out of control in the best way.

THE WISDOM OF THE CROWD

What are some methods you use to make people feel appreciated?

> I was talking with a client yesterday about how Peloton and safe driving apps have people coming back for more because of the 'free badges' you win from working out, working hard, or driving safely. Yes, it's awesome (and I am totally sucked into both of these programs), however, there is no need to invest money in an app. Saying thank you, congrats, and giving public praise is free! Make a sticky note, practice, and make it part of your daily routine.

—Jennifer Tankanow, Co-founder and VP of JointPivot

> If I don't recognize people when they do good work, how much less will they hear me if I need to offer anything other than praise. If I make a practice of catching people doing things 'right' I am able to show how everyone contributes.

—Evans Kerrigan, CEO and Co-Founder, Integris Performance Advisors, and Co-Author of *Solving the People Problem*

> Giving credit where due is one of the four foundations of good supervisory relationships as set out in Training

Within Industry's (TWI's) Job Relations module. When asked why people leave their job, the most common reason given is the bad relationship with their boss, including their efforts being under-appreciated. I had a client go from 60% annual staff turnover to 10% annual turnover in just four months when the supervisors started following those four foundations. Their biggest behavioral change was giving credit to people.

—Hugh Alley, Author of *Becoming the Supervisor*

REFLECTIONS

Most people have good intentions, yet worklife can be overwhelmingly fast-paced and all-consuming. Stopping, even for a moment, takes intention and time. But it's a false sense of economy to save time by keeping your head down and missing the contributions of those around you. You forge connections and strengthen relationships that way. It's an indispensable activity.

INK MAKES YOU THINK

- Is there someone or some people you haven't recognized lately?
- What might you say to them? You can email it, text it, or simply say it.
- What do you think will happen?

---

1. Daniel Pink, *Drive: The Surprising Truth About What Motivates Us* (Riverhead Books, 2009)

35

HELP OTHERS NAVIGATE THE UNKNOWN

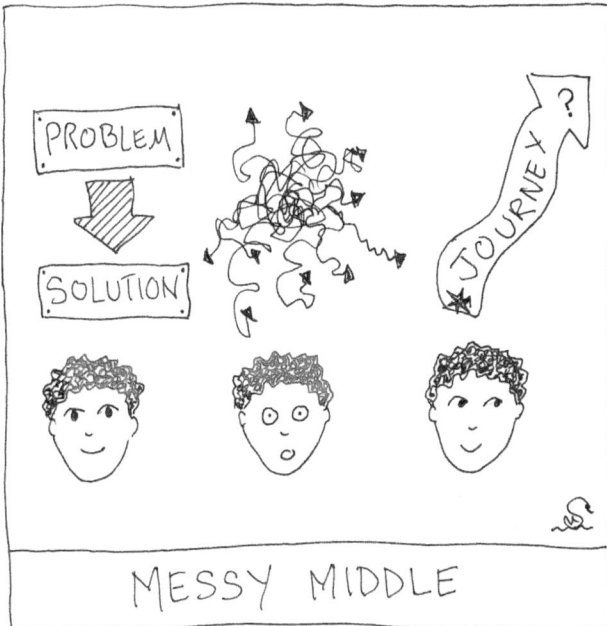

THE MESSY MIDDLE IS THAT PLACE OF UNCERTAINTY FOR PEOPLE TRYING TO SOLVE PROBLEMS.

They often start off confident of an issue and how to solve it. Then, if they get some guidance, they begin investigating the process, asking questions, collecting data, and that's when things often lose their clarity. The expanding reality may not warrant the original solution, which breeds self-doubt. Helping people travel through the messy middle means knowing they're heading there.

"The problem is we need credit card machines on all the delivery trucks!" The finance manager was sure she knew why the company was delivering partial orders of appliances. Customers complained that receiving only a refrigerator and a stove, without the dishwasher, meant having to reschedule installation. They were justifiably mad, and she knew the root cause was not being able to handle cash-on-delivery orders.

Could there be other root causes? It turned out that only 10% of the partial deliveries were due to customers not being able to pay on delivery. The other 90% were due to appliances going on backorder. She'd already done the research on installing credit card machines in the trucks—it seemed so obvious. She was deflated by the conflicting data. She was in the messy middle.

Once she took it all in, the remedy was to contact customers when any part of their order went on backorder. They added a step to give them the option of substituting a different brand or accepting a partial order. The interim calls to the customers took time, but the extra step paled in comparison to the costs of purchasing and installing the credit card machines. She got there, she acknowledged the error of jumping to a solution, and she knew she'd have to continue battling that instinct.

If you've been in the business—any business—for a while, it's easy to forget how foggy things seem to beginners. They come in with premature conclusions, and they feel good about what they're offering. They haven't done the analysis, but they describe their ideas with pride. When you push back, you challenge them to rethink their positions, leaving them with a sense of loss. You take away their clarity and push them into the haze.

There are other terms that capture the messy middle like, "learning is uncomfortable." What helps is to lend confidence to people by meeting them where they are. The finance manager was so sure she'd solved the problem. What helped was to ask her if there could be any other root causes. She did the work and successfully challenged her own assumptions. Stepping back from predetermined outcomes frees people up to explore and experiment. Scary, but a path to discovery.

It helps to remind people of the natural progression of learning. And the gray areas aren't restricted to newbies. We all wade through fog, if we're truly going to learn anything new. Prepare for uncertainty, but push ahead into the unknown. You can support those you work with as they bounce around through the process and gain awareness of what they don't know.

———

THE WISDOM OF THE CROWD

How do you support people as they navigate the messy middle?

> A mentor of mine once counseled me to 'follow the data.' Let the data be your guide, rather than pre-supposing solutions before truly understanding the situation and causes. When in the messy middle, data —whether in the form of information or analysis—are ideally objective and can be that helpful guide. Upfront, a good problem statement can also help get learners off on the right foot. If we can coach them to focus only on the issue, magnitude, gap and impact, while refraining from including any reference to assumptions, causes, or

potential solutions, then they may be more open to 'following the data' to see where it takes them.

—Terrance P. Callanan, Lean Six Sigma Consultant

I remind my teams that jumping to a solution is a faster approach that makes management happy because they see immediate action being taken. However, management ultimately wants effective solutions, and none of us wants to waste time and money on something that won't work. Instead of delaying real results, let's take the extra time now to dig deep into the issue. We will come up with a more effective solution, even if it takes a little longer to accomplish. That seems to help them mentally prepare for the 'messy middle.'

—Brion Hurley, Lean Six Sigma Master Black Belt, and Author of *Lean Six Sigma for Good*

Asking "What do you need to learn next, and what is something you could do in 20 minutes that would help you learn it?" has been a very helpful question for me at this stage of the process. It acknowledges that not knowing is normal, and has them focus on identifying a small step they can take. That lets them see progress, and it helps them see that they don't have to solve it all in one go. I learned this technique in the context of coaching people in the Toyota Kata, with thanks to Mark Rosenthal, but I've found it has much wider application.

—Hugh Alley, Author of *Becoming the Supervisor*

REFLECTIONS

The Messy Middle is not a bad thing. It's proof that you're learning and growing. The key is to have a guide who cares that you "arrive alive." Someone who's interested in you making it through the fog. People need help and guidance in different ways, so it helps to figure out what support they're looking for. It might not be enough to ask "how can I help." When people are in the fog, they often can't articulate what that is. You can switch up your questions to get them to form a picture of help by asking, 'If I were helping you, what would you see me doing?'"

INK MAKES YOU THINK

- Think of a time you were working with someone who was feeling unsure. What kind of help might they have needed?
- Going forward, how could you ensure a person knows you're vested in their success?
- What might you say to them?

36

GIVE NEW LEADERS A FIGHTING CHANCE

CONGRATS! YOU'RE THE BOSS NOW!

"CONGRATS, YOU'RE THE BOSS NOW!"

Those words bring back the excitement of getting promoted to Production Manager. To be 25 years old and working at an Apple II software startup in Emeryville, California, felt like a junior pinnacle. Then it got a bit rocky.

When they first hired me, I felt lucky to land a job in tech support. Helping customers with complex configurations, developing standard responses to common issues, and testing printers and other hardware with our software was intensely satisfying. It was fun "burning eproms," although don't ask me what that means now.

As the firm grew, my work on customer communications got me promoted to the tech-writing team. Our software manuals—back when that meant bound things you held in your hands—were glossy and hip. As tech writers we were allowed to use our own voice and we were a salty bunch. Apple had recently debuted the Macintosh, which ushered in desktop publishing. That meant we could write, lay out, and produce all of our user manuals. It was a blast.

From there they catapulted me to head of production. That meant overseeing the programmers, beta testers, and tech writers. That's when things changed. The work was absorbing, but I had ceased to be "one of the guys." One casualty was my friendship with the man who hired me. We had bonded over being the only east-coasters in this California start-up (no one else seemed capable of driving in the rain). As soon as he started reporting to me, our connection began to fray. It was baffling and lonely.

Over the years, I've seen others follow a similar path. There are corporate ladders with established rungs. If people are good at what they do, the typical next step is to put them in charge of others. It may be the only way leadership sees to keep and reward talent. The assumption seems to be that if you excel at your craft you'll be equally good at managing people. But there's a chasm between technical and interpersonal skills. It's a nebulous place where people struggle and fail.

I spoke with Hugh Alley, author of *Becoming the Supervisor,* about what he's seen as key success factors. He described five core skills necessary for people to succeed as leaders.

They must be able to:

1. Instruct
2. Deal with performance not meeting expectations
3. Improve methods
4. Set priorities
5. Listen

If they can do these five things passably well, they'll succeed. Colleagues and management can identify which of these core skills your role needs most at the moment. Looking back, our scrappy start-up hadn't developed a way to handle performance issues. That core skill eluded me. Luckily there were generous mentors at my next career stop. They helped me gain skills and a lot more empathy for nascent leaders.

———

THE WISDOM OF THE CROWD

What was your first leadership experience like? If you struggled, what helped?

> We often take a super worker and turn them into a supervisor thinking the required skills are the same. This is probably one of the most under-supported role changes in the workforce.
>
> —Jamie Flinchbaugh, Author of *People Solve Problems*

My first real adult leader role was for an internship program in our department. Here is what I remember learning:

Tell the 'why': People you lead will never understand the value of what they are doing if you skip this.

Listen: And then actually implement a few things you heard. Show people they matter.

Chill out: It's okay if they make mistakes. It's a part of the learning process.

Watch those around you. Identify the leadership qualities you value and want to emulate.

Great question for everyone's leadership journey!

—Jennifer Tankanow, Co-Founder and VP of JointPivot

Lead by example. I never climbed to the boss's chair. Instead I stayed with the team and spent time training and working on the floor and on the battlefield. Thanks to my team I achieved the 'Rookie Manager of the Year' and 'Manager of the Year.' Many of my colleagues got promoted too.

—Manuel Drasdo, Export, Lean, Logistics & Supply Chain Management

REFLECTIONS

People are promoted at a young age, and then decades can pass before they get any leadership training.

Organizations often fail to support and prepare new leaders for the "managing others" side of the equation. No one is born with those skills; they require education, practice and guidance. Delegation is essential to good leadership, so there's no need to go it alone. Finding and enlisting collaborators in your journey is essential. Offering guidance and assistance to others new at leadership is both kind and useful.

INK MAKES YOU THINK

- Think of a time someone (maybe you) experienced failure.
- What words of advice or support might have helped them or you?
- What do you think the reaction would have been?

Practice those words as they may come in useful soon.

37

GO FROM SETBACK TO INSIGHT

WHAT HAVE YOU LEARNED FROM FAILURE? HAVE YOU EVER EXPERIENCED WHAT YOU CONSIDERED FAILURE?

Experiencing what felt like a crushing defeat over twenty years ago is hard to forget. We were rolling out a companywide continuous improvement effort for a multinational hotel chain in a stunning European resort. United States leadership and all the European area directors were in attendance.

The centerpiece of the conference, in terms of changing the hearts and minds of the European leadership, was a full-day simulation. It was a proof-of-concept event that I'd built specifically for them. It had gone so well during the US rollout, that the Wall Street Journal quoted the CEO on its success. We assumed that since it was well-received in the U.S., we'd enjoy another round of success.

But things didn't go as planned. Jet lag left me with twenty-four hours of sleep deprivation. The consultant assigned to assist me didn't know his role. Then the foreign area directors turned. Some of them weren't happy about having to learn a new model, and they worked steadily to undermine the process. My colleagues used to claim that you couldn't "break" the simulation since whatever the outcome, there was learning to be had. Well, on that day, and in my case, it broke.

The other simulation sessions had gone well, so the multi-day event continued apace. Upon finally joining the consulting team the next day, my face confirmed what they'd heard. In an effort to shake me loose from my misery, one of them asked, "Do you mean to say you've *never* bombed before?" He smiled. Then he entertained me with stories of his own epic takedowns. He made me laugh, which was a much better look than my flat guise of remorse. I've never forgotten that kindness, and decades later we're still connected.

During the follow-up, the client was gracious and worked to see if they had played a role in the outcome of the rogue group. They apologized for not having supported me better. They threw me right back into the fray to run the next few events, and we continued to enjoy a strong working relationship for decades. It reminds me of how generous people can be, and the grace we can extend to others. People fail all the time in small and spectacular ways, and what matters is how you react.

Depending on the culture, when things don't go as planned, people can become defensive and dishonest. Events can result in blame, and a sense of shame. Yet failing to succeed is one of the outcomes of *trying* to succeed. It's evidence that you don't understand your system well enough—what you were expecting didn't happen. The next step is to dig in to find out what's missing in your understanding.

Failure is a loaded word. Nelson Mandela found a way to operate without it, "I never lose. I win or learn." If you want people to try and learn, it has to be okay to fall short. Failure only happens if we learn nothing from it.

———

THE WISDOM OF THE CROWD

What have you learned from failure?

> I just read something[1] that said we don't learn from failure because we get too tied up in self-criticism and can't see our way out. We *do* however learn from other people's failure because it doesn't feel personal. Fascinating!
>
> —Dorsey Sherman, MHSA, ACC, and President of Modèle Consulting

> I have experienced failure many times. But over the last two years, I decided to think about experimenting vs.

failure. Instead of thinking that we did something wrong, we are learning.

—Lauren Hisey, Continuous Business Process Improvement Consultant and Speaker

I've learned there's always a tomorrow. My mentor, John Maxwell shares that we 'fail forward,' and 'sometimes we win and sometimes we learn (learn instead of fail).' I'm also encouraged to remember that failure is an event and not a person. Most growth and development begin from the inside out and failure is just the opportunity for an additional stretch-reflect-and-grow moment.

—Rick Foreman, John Maxwell Team Certified Coach-Trainer-Speaker

REFLECTIONS

Your ability to reframe "failure" as an outcome that wasn't expected can help a lot. It still may take time for a person to get over the torment of a perceived loss and see any benefit. There's an adage that tragedy plus time equals comedy. It can take a while to get to the comedy. Focus on why the performance was different from what they expected and how they can learn from it. That's the benefit of the inevitable mishaps of any journey. And maybe you can offer up a joke or two.

INK MAKES YOU THINK

- Are you aware of someone who did not perform as they expected?
- In what way could you help them find what they missed in their understanding of the situation?

- What would you say?
- How might they react?

Remember, they may perceive themselves as having failed, and your words can hasten their constructive journey.

---

1. https://characterlab.org/tips-of-the-week/oops/

38

LAY A PATH FOR OTHERS

ARE YOU IN THE WAY? MAYBE THE BETTER QUESTION IS WHETHER YOU'RE OPENING A PATH FOR OTHERS.

For me it happened in a fun way during a family yard-work party. These have become yearly get-togethers, which are ostensibly a gift for my mother. Each year an ever-expanding crew shows up to weed, whack, rake, clip, plug roof holes, fix the deck, and you get the idea. The transformations are breathtaking.

In the early days, me and my three-page master chore list formed the chief bottleneck. As each car pulled into the driveway, friends peppered me with questions, "what's on the list?," "where should I go?" Answering questions left me unable to get much done which was frustrating, because it was fun!

The answer was to turn my mother's driveway into a visual workplace. My day job remains a mystery to my family but a Kanban Board doesn't need much explaining. Kanban is "signboard" in Japanese, and the setup is fairly intuitive. There are usually three columns labeled "To Do," "Doing," and "Done." You move items from left to right as you decide what to work on, work on it, and then finish the task. These can be digital or physical and populated by sticky notes.

Although the installation of my flipchart under the basketball hoop raised eyebrows, people had no trouble assessing the board, finding the job they wanted to work on, and then heading out into the yard. "Chainsaw fallen trees" was a big seller given a recent Nor'easter. The second year of the Kanban Board turned slightly mutinous.

Having engaged in some chores the year before that they wished they hadn't—the basement is a bit scary—the categories changed to "Maybe," "It's On," and "So Done!" I lost control of what went up on the board. Tasks labeled "eat pizza" and "drink beer" migrated into the "It's On" column. A skull and crossbones appeared on another task that involved crawling under the deck.

As the day came to a close and pizza and beer appeared (pizza appeared, the beer was not new). Everyone milled around the driveway, seemingly waiting for instruction. While I was deciding whether to say something, one of my sisters, a landscaper by trade, got ahead of me and stood next to the board. Plucking a note from the "On It" section she checked to see what we'd finished. "Did someone trim the ewe bush?"

"So Done!" the crowd yelled back. This call and response continued until she'd moved all the sticky notes—a strangely satisfying activity —into the "So Done!" section. Watching my sister own the Kanban Board was a joyous moment for me. The board was completed, the crowd was unruly, and mother hugged everyone while her rescue dog Scrappy barked non-stop. It was a huge success, and my days as chief bottleneck were long over.

Have you ever had the opportunity to remove yourself and open a path for others? A chance to find the right tools, offer the right resources to shift authority so people can find their own way? Removing yourself might create a happy opening.

––––––––

THE WISDOM OF THE CROWD

Have you ever discovered that your best contribution was getting out of the way?

> I once had a wonderful manager who taught me that the true role of a leader is to build a great team and then get out of their way. He made it clear that he expected us to do the same with our teams. If he caught a whiff of us micromanaging people he would gently remind us that we were there to provide direction, to inspire, and to support when needed. *Not* to suffocate our people or squash their learning opportunities. I

needed a few reminders early on, but soon learned to let go. It was liberating—for us all.

—Gemma Jones, Improvement Coach, Founder of SPARK Improvement Ltd.

The owner of the consultancy firm where I just started, brought me in on a meeting with the executive team of one of our clients. Impressed by the opportunity and eager to show them what I was made of, I "hijacked" the conversation. Every time my "boss" asked a question, I joined in and shared my insights, sometimes before the client could. My boss gave me (literally) one of the most impactful learning opportunities of my career: he kicked me in the shins! He silenced me and created room for the clients to tell their story and take ownership. We were just there to listen and facilitate the process, I discovered.

—Arnout Orelio, Author of *Lean Thinking in Health Care*

During the course of coaching and training others to use Lean and Lean Six Sigma Tools, I am frequently pleased to see how well my students take hold of the concepts. After witnessing just a few examples that I have presented to them, they turn around and reach surprising levels of accomplishment through doing their projects on their own. And in completing these projects, they engage others and become teachers themselves. It is quite gratifying to see that happen.

—Jerry M. Wright, PE, MBA, CEO and President, LEANwRIGHT

REFLECTIONS

There are lots of reasons to be in charge, and it's often the right thing to do. The trick is to ask yourself if there's a way to liberate yourself and empower others. Does the task require a leader? Given the right resources, could the group self govern? When people own their own tools and get the freedom to make things better, they are more likely to enjoy the opportunity. They may even add a reward system—potentially more sophisticated than pizza and beer.

INK MAKES YOU THINK

- Think of some area or task you currently manage.
- Could it be handled differently or by others?
- Are you truly necessary?
- How could you pave the way for others?
- What would that look like?

39

BE A LEADER PEOPLE WANT TO FOLLOW

RBG

RUTH
BADER
GINSBURG

FIGHT FOR THE THINGS
YOU CARE ABOUT

"FIGHT FOR THE THINGS YOU CARE ABOUT."

The second half of Ruth Bader Ginsburg's quote is, "But do it in a way that will lead others to join you." It's that second sentence that resonates.

Fight—but invite. That means you must consider yourself a leader.

While helping a nurse with her improvement project, she told me she was concerned that the nurses in her unit didn't see any reason to fix the documentation process. She was frustrated because they weren't grasping the issue that was so clear to her. She had a measurable problem—missing information. She knew her solution—a new capture method—would work. She was considering going to her manager to mandate the change, and she wanted to know what I thought. What I *thought* was that she might achieve some compliance. What I *thought* was that she should prepare to lose a few friends.

You are often an agent of change, and you might be helping others hone their ability to usher in change. Part of that process involves unearthing data that makes the case for change. But remember, facts and data can fail to move hearts and minds. You need to invite people to join you in the journey—and consider what that invitation looks like.

If you fail to embrace the leadership aspects of your role, you might feel like a lone voice in the wilderness. Don't sell yourself short. Others are watching and listening to you. What you do and what you say will either cause people to follow or leave you to walk a lonely path. You need to own your role.

Which brings us back to the invitation. How might the team leader encourage the other nurses to come along with her? Where are the opportunities? Did she know why the other nurses failed to see the issues that she was witnessing? She didn't. Could she think of any questions to ask them that would help her understand their position? She could.

She realized she hadn't walked the process with them. She'd neglected to ask them about pain points from their perspective. She had approached her colleagues *after* she'd come up with a solution, not before. She set her sights on restarting the conversation. Begin at the very beginning. The discussions might lead in another direction. Her ideas might not survive, and she was open to that.

———

THE WISDOM OF THE CROWD

Are others following you? How do you encourage them to join you?

> We are all leaders. Others imitate and model how they act, react, and interact by watching and listening to what you do. Act, speak, and interact kindly. You can choose to lead with kindness through difficult times and difficult situations. We all need to work on creating a kinder world. Failures of leadership and failures of kindness lead to failures for all of us.
>
> —Karyn Ross, Activator and Author of *The Kind Leader*

> I learned that I need to be my authentic self and, in turn, I hope I lead others to do the same. Yes, I'm wacky and I want to bring the fun, but when I was a young professional I thought I wouldn't be taken seriously. I grew tired of putting on the subdued mask. Now, if people don't like what I bring, they can find their own people ... and I say that with love.
>
> —Tracy O'Rourke, Co-Author of *The Problem-Solver's Toolkit*

People want to follow people who genuinely care about them. I know I do! In my opinion, if you want people to take action, start by taking action yourself and truly, authentically, caring for others. Not that caring-because-you-want-something stuff. The real deal! It makes you a better leader ... a better coach ... a better person.

—Stephanie Feger, Author of *Make Your Author emPact*

REFLECTIONS

This is one of the harder lessons in life. One that seems in a constant state of education. Advocating for what's right often seems self-evident. But the part where others listen to you is less so. You often get stuck on the notion of *buy-in* which translates to *selling* something that the other person had no involvement in and didn't ask for. What's far more powerful is ownership. What's the pathway for others to own and become a part of the journey? You have inquiry, kindness, repetition, and reflection. It's a constant cycle and you need to lead with intent. Make sure the invitation is ... inviting.

INK MAKES YOU THINK

- Are you coaching yourself or others on how to sell your ideas?
- How might you switch the focus from getting buy-in to inviting ownership?
- What would that different approach look like?

Remember, you are modeling the way.

40

UNITE YOUR TRIBES

SILOS HAPPEN

SILOS HAPPEN WITHOUT EFFORT—IT TAKES NOTHING FOR US TO CONSTRUCT REAL AND VIRTUAL WALLS BETWEEN NATURAL GROUPS.

As a part of a seven-person company, as small as we were, it was clear we had silos. Sometimes the signal was a simple acronym. A member of our two-man marketing team referenced the LCV. They were happy to explain the importance of Lifetime Customer Value—and seven syllables down to three feels like a win—but our paths were diverging.

If you work closely with others you develop your own shorthand. Acronyms are the most obvious private "language" but other short-cuts creep in. Listening to a client from talent acquisition refer to "recs" it was unclear whether they meant requisitions, requirements, or recommendations. We cleared it up, but it's a process.

There are organizations where silos are encouraged as a form of internal competition. Separate divisions stockpile information for perceived gain. That seems depressingly underhanded, and the reality is much more benign. Efficiency dictates that we can't be in constant conversation with an entire workforce. To "cc" or copy hordes of people on an email in the name of sharing is a modern-day cruelty. On the other hand, if we fail to stay connected, then we inevitably transform into "us" and "them" which are the hallmarks of a destructive, blame culture.

Humans are tribal, and silos are tribes. It takes work to bridge the divides that crop up and solidify over time. Organizations pull people together because we can accomplish more in concert with each other. If we can find ways to keep connected, we are capable of greatness. On a project level, exciting breakthroughs happen during simple Process Walks. People within the same process get together and learn about each other. Yet there's a larger entity that needs to stay in the conversation.

———

THE WISDOM OF THE CROWD

What have you seen that helps break down organizational silos?

> As you say, silos are tribes—natural human patterns of belonging. Breaking them down then would mean forcing something unnatural. So perhaps re-connecting is a term that can help the effort? My go-to method for reconnecting is A3 thinking. It has worked well by bringing cross-functional assumptions to the surface (including clarifying acronyms) and aligning efforts with the end customer in mind. I've seen A3s help reconnect the most tribally-diverse teams by forming internal customer-supplier relationships.

—Sam Yankelevitch, Author of *Walking the Invisible Gemba*

> I agree that silos naturally develop in organizations and that it takes a lot of work to bridge the divides. I think there are plenty of actions that can build those bridges. My top three are: 1. Cross departmental mentoring programs, 2. Cross departmental value stream/process mapping and project work, and 3. Social and sports clubs (Sometimes the informal approach works really well).

—Catherine McDonald, Organisational Behaviour, Lean, and Leadership Coach at MCD Consulting

> Change the organizational structure from functional silos to cross-functional value stream teams that have the talent and resources to go from customer inquiry to delivery. There is no law, and it was not written on the back of Moses' tablets, that you must organize the

company by function. Lots of lean companies organize by value streams.

—Bill Waddell, Global Restructuring Leadership

REFLECTIONS

The need to actively connect people is clear. As organizations grow, people become less connected to the original vision. When asked, most people can't recite the mission statement. A refresh on why the company exists helps, and from there an effort to showcase where people share goals—like on-time delivery—across departments where possible. Cross-department Process Walks can educate and connect at strategic levels. There's also the less corporate angle of getting together to play a game of bocce or some group Wordle. Disparate groups can connect, they simply need rituals to reinforce their common bonds.

INK MAKES YOU THINK

- What silo are you a part of?
- What silos are you disconnected from?
- Who could you reach out to in order to invest in some formal connection?
- What might result from that connection?

41

CREATE THE TIES THAT BIND YOU TO COMMUNITY

COMMUNITY!

COMMUNITY! WHO YA GONNA CALL?

That's an obvious callback from an '80s comedy ... *Ghostbusters*! Consider the question in a larger sense. When you're struggling with a persistently thorny issue or you're wrestling with a brand new situation, who do you reach out to? Are you stronger on strategy and need help with tech issues? Are you venturing into a new area and need some advice from a veteran? Who is in your network and how do you manage it?

My networks are surprisingly diverse and often happenstance; clients who've become friends, a Lean women's group on LinkedIn, a sports team from my 20s, most of the guests from a friend's wedding that took place seventeen years ago, consultants I've worked with, and countless other groups. We may not speak for a bit, but we reappear for each other with ease.

Whatever your network is, outside events can profoundly affect it. People reported that the COVID-19 pandemic both shrank their world and expanded it. With limited ability to meet and gather, everyone was forced into video calls. Although many experienced "Zoom-fatigue," and relished the opportunity to meet in person, our ability to stay connected gets demonstrably better with expanding remote options.

Without the expectation of being in person, you can attend more meetings. Without the need for transportation, you've got more time to connect. Is your network ad-hoc? Do you know people from different industries who help you stay current? Are there people you call simply for sanity checks?

And with the opportunity for limitless meetups comes the responsibility to maintain those connections. According to British anthropologist Robin Dunbar[1], we're capable of maintaining relationships with about one-hundred and fifty people. We can have around five hundred acquaintances, and then people slip through the cracks.

Should you go to the reunion? Can you attend that conference? Whether online or in-person, there are events providing openings to reconnect and solidify relationships across the board. Your networks help you navigate the unknown and keep you part of a larger whole.

Human beings have heart, grit, and massive generosity. It's important to maintain the bonds you've formed and build from there. Regardless of the nature of your network, remember to view it as a living thing.

———

THE WISDOM OF THE CROWD

How do you build and maintain your network?

> Through the COVID-19 pandemic I, thankfully, found myself increasingly connected to various global communities, all united online. Zoom and Teams became my workspace and I steadily built strong relationships with a network of people across the world. The Kata community is particularly generous and open to newcomers, and this in turn encourages members to contribute and share. It's a virtuous circle which attracts and retains people and builds a spirit of innovation, support and teamwork.
>
> —Gemma Jones, Improvement Coach and Founder of SPARK Improvement Ltd.

> Building relationships and creating community is a must for a leader and business owner. I have two mastermind groups that I am part of with women who are in the continuous improvement space and one in the leadership and equity space. Both have been life-changing. That community stretches to individual rela-

tionships with other entrepreneurs from all over the world. I could not do life without those essential connections, and I look to build and add more community daily. I encourage everyone to find multiple individuals and groups that feed them and that they can also give to. I mentor and have a group for that as well. These groups sustain and support me when I am on a high or need support in staying encouraged. Community is life-changing and is necessary for all of us.

—Kim Crowder, Certified in Diversity, Equity, and Lean Six Sigma Leadership, and CEO and Founder of Kim Crowder Consulting

Building relationships is essential for growing as a human being. Yet oftentimes, our relationships are limited to our families, geographical locations, interests, and professions. After a certain age, it's not easy to allow new people into our circles. In December of 2019, I embarked on an intentional experience to meet 100 new people for lunch—to learn more about myself, others, and the world. This experience turned virtual and therefore international. I met 100 women and men from nine countries, across four continents, from different backgrounds and career paths, who held different mental models and beliefs from mine. It completely changed the trajectory of my life. I recommend it to anyone who wants to get out of their comfort zone, build a broader and more nuanced life perspective, and learn to connect deeply with themselves and others.

—Lili Boyanova Hugh, Founder of Wholeheartedlead & Leader at the Center for a Loving Workplace

REFLECTIONS

Without leaving home, you're able to connect with an innovative, expansive, and supportive group of people. Whether in person or remotely, there is both the need to build your network and the work of maintaining those bonds. Keep in mind the limited number of connections you can maintain. There's a balancing act that is worth establishing.

INK MAKES YOU THINK

- Who have you formed connections with?
- Where have you lost connection?
- What groups have you joined?
- What group could you start?

Make the call.

---

1. https://www.bbc.com/future/article/20191001-dunbars-number-why-we-can-only-maintain-150-relationships

TREAT PEOPLE WITH RESPECT—LOOKING BACK

Part Five

You spend most of your days inside your own head. Without prompting, you might fail to reflect on what's happening for those in your orbit. Whether you're aware or not, people are taking cues from you on a regular basis. Being more cognizant and intentional about what they see and hear from you will help both them and you. Your triumphs are dependent on the success of those you lead. You are vocationally intertwined with others.

Reflect on what you want to change about how you treat those around you. Do you have new questions to ask? Are you looking for opportunities to sing the praises of others? Do you have some ideas of how to support someone newly promoted?

KEY POINTS SUMMARY

34. Be Generous in Your Praise
People get used to going unnoticed so acknowledging their accomplishments has a big impact on their self-esteem, motivation, and interest in helping you.

35. Help Others Navigate the Unknown
Learning is uncomfortable, and learners need a caring hand to see them through the messiness of getting educated.

36. Give New Leaders a Fighting Chance
Ensure the people who get promoted get the preparation they need so they have a shot at success.

37. Go from Setback to Insight
You're poised to help others learn from failure by supporting them through their perceived losses.

38. Lay a Path for Others
Are you necessary to the task at hand? Could you clear a path for other leaders?

39. Be a Leader People Want to Follow
You are a change agent, and you're responsible for shepherding other change agents—remember to check who's following.

40. Unite Your Tribes
Organizational success leads to growth, and growth increases the distance between people so you have to actively reach across departmental boundaries.

41. Create the Ties that Bind You To Community
Your network is essential to your success—are you nurturing your vital connections?

UP NEXT

When airlines instruct us on what to do in the event of a crash—if they have our attention—they stress the need for parents to put their oxygen masks on first, before placing them on children. The same holds true for leaders. It's easy to think of others and what "oxygen" means for them. It's not always easy to consider that for ourselves, but it's essential to our ability to navigate change. We'll cover our mindsets regarding ourselves next.

.

Part Six

RESPECT YOURSELF

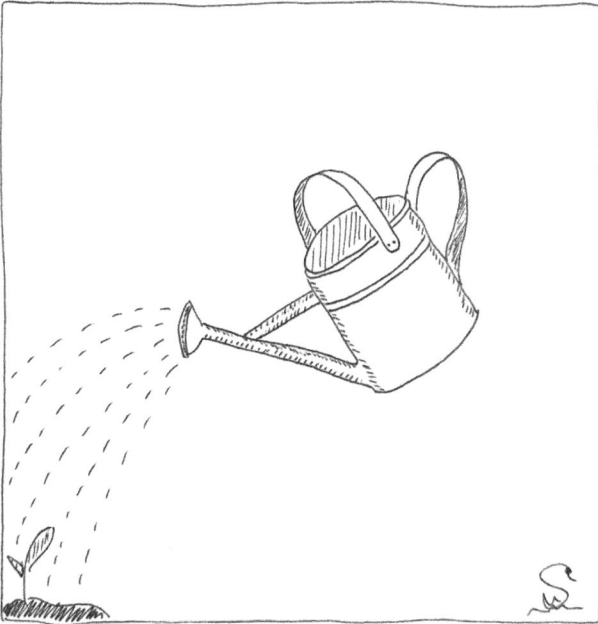

You have an outward-facing journey as you guide people you work with.

There's your behavior—what people see you do. You've also got an inner journey that drives those actions. And, even though you spend most of your time inside your own head, that doesn't mean you do it efficiently or effectively. There's waste in those neural networks. You deserve better.

With a willing chorus of compatriots, you'll learn how others navigate the mindset of the change agent, and benefit from their insights.

42. Morph Gaffes into Gems
How to stay flexible in the moment.

43. Contend with Yourself Instead of Others
The cost of seeing yourself as less-than.

44. Do the Thing You Fear
How to recognize "good fear."

45. Give Your Gifts to Yourself
What can you gain from your own advice?

46. Ditch the Shoe Once It No Longer Fits
Progress requires movement regardless of the direction.

47. Use Humor, It's Contagious
Being able to laugh at yourself is a leadership asset.

48. Refer Authority and Grow Leaders
Delegation is key to leadership.

49. Participate! Culture is a Contact Sport
Heed the toxic warning signs.

50. Assume Permission Granted

What if you just did it?

42

MORPH GAFFES INTO GEMS

YEARS AGO, I FOUND A BUMPER STICKER THAT READ, "IMPROVISE & OVERCOME."

Having bought two, the message survived a rear-ender and new bumper. When it was time to sell the car, the internet revealed dozens of sites where you could invent and order your own stickers. Handing them out at the end of workshops helped me reinforce in everyone's minds that even the best laid plans go awry. Participants learn well-documented ways to solve problems, but that doesn't guarantee they get what they plan for.

You're running a brainstorming session, but it's Friday afternoon and everyone is too fried to come up with new ideas. You prepared a colorful digital whiteboard where teams can collaborate remotely, but the company doesn't allow external software, so you have to scrap it. You arranged a working session to redesign a form only to discover you need permission from the "Forms" Department, and you don't have it. Maybe you already have the answer and your only job is to guide everyone to the solution. But they're not buying it.

As your efforts and plans go pear-shaped (visually enjoyable, albeit baffling, British slang for "go wrong), you're faced with some choices, and most likely a series of unpleasant emotions. There's the sinking feeling of "what now?" You might have a fleeting sense of frustration, but it helps to remember you also have freedom. Since you can't do what you planned to do, you get to make something up—you get to improvise.

Performing on stage taught me that improvisers are most captivating when embracing mistakes. It's key to listen carefully because slip-ups are gold. You benefit by embracing that same mindset on the job. Stay attuned to what others bring to the conversation. When someone answers your question in a way you weren't ready for, you have an opportunity to reflect on the gap. Use it to spark unexpected dialogue. Take a chance on that exchange.

And if it's your mistake, what can you learn from those affected?

MORPH GAFFES INTO GEMS • 229

If you're working with colleagues, see how they'd solve the problem. Your sense of control is often an illusion. "Getting it right" can prevent you from staying attentive to what is happening around you. If you're bent on perfection, you lose the advantage of flexibility. Instead of, "I don't want any surprises," what if you thought, "How can I take advantage of the element of surprise?"

It makes things more interesting for all involved. It's a skill and a mindset worth practicing.

———

THE WISDOM OF THE CROWD

What are some techniques you use to come prepared but stay flexible?

> When things don't go the way I had expected, I try to ask myself, "What am I learning here?" I get curious (not always easy to do!). When things really go awry, I think to myself, I might as well enjoy the rollercoaster! I try to find humor in the situation.
>
> —Sonia Singh, Principal & Executive Coach at SS International

> I tend to ask a lot of questions to engage people in meetings and classrooms. Anytime you ask questions, you let go of some element of control and let others have more impact. Asking questions can be scary because of that element of surprise, but it's worth it.
>
> —Tracy O'Rourke, Co-Author of *The Problem-Solver's Toolkit*

> For me, a trick I learned very early on was to *not* memorize a script for what I wanted to say. I trained myself instead to get really comfy with 360 degrees of a topic, so that my ability to speak on the fly, adapt to the circumstances, and feel the room/audience was most familiar.

—Alyssa Elliott, Process Improvement Coach

REFLECTIONS

There's no end to hairy derailments and curveballs coming your way. Stay mindful of the impact on yourself, and try to understand what's happening for others. And whether digital or physical, post-it notes, duct tape, and sharpie pens might see you through. It's not always easy to stay curious, but it helps if you pepper your approach with humor and humility. People are empathetic when you're human. Remember, there's something inviting about leaders who are slightly less polished. They make way for unguarded moments. Embrace the flaw and react to what's happening in the room. Always be reading the situation.

INK MAKES YOU THINK

- What's one way you can prepare yourself for improvisation?
- Write it down.
- What might come of it?

Now improvise and overcome.

43

CONTEND WITH YOURSELF INSTEAD OF OTHERS

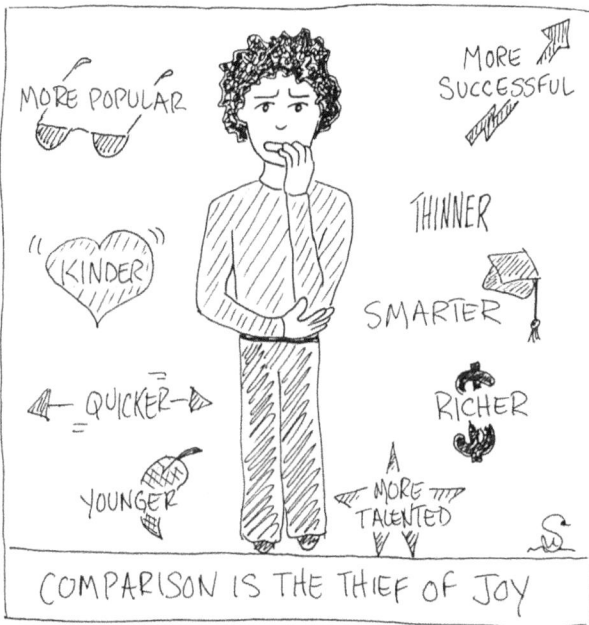

COMPARISON IS THE THIEF OF JOY. ENVY AND JEALOUSY FEEL DISHONORABLE, YET THEY'RE INTENSELY HUMAN.

Occasionally a brave soul will acknowledge their struggles with feeling less-than. But as much as we *get* intellectually that comparison is pointless, we often succumb to fear when someone else succeeds.

This reminded me of my stepfather's story about attending his thirty-fifth college reunion. In the buffet line he overheard two classmates discussing their gigantic, six-figure salaries. It dawned on him that every single member of his class likely made more money—a lot more—than he did. He was silent for a beat. "But I could still kick their asses."

I love that story for so many reasons. He was funny! And yes, he was a big man and he'd been a stellar athlete (invited to join the Baltimore Orioles' farm team) so there's some truth to his joke—a humor essential. More important, his ability to laugh at himself in that moment was part of what made him a great man. Standing in that buffet line, he may have felt pangs of regret. He made precious little money in his lifetime—but he left a stunning legacy.

He dedicated his life to co-founding and running an alternative reform school. He became, in his words, a professional father figure. He rerouted decades of teenage criminals into useful lives. There are books, TV specials, and other evidence of his impact, but that's not why he did what he did. The option to give in and compare himself to others more financially successful was always at hand, and he chose to kick its ass instead.

It's a lesson that requires perpetual learning. If you can't stop the comparison, it helps to at least acknowledge you're doing it. In those moments, rest assured there's someone feeling the same way about you. Like my stepfather, you've got the opportunity to focus on something positive in yourself.

We are all practiced in the fine art of comparison. You can always find someone "better than." Always. It helps to reflect on your super-powers—what you bring to the party—and to have a sense of humor.

———

THE WISDOM OF THE CROWD

How do you escape the impulse to compare yourself to others?

> In the book, *The Midnight Library,* by Matt Haig (which seems an odd reference), the woman talks about life as a swim meet. She said you focus on your own time, and you stay in your lane. If you turn your head to find out where other people are, you will slow down, well up with some type of unproductive emotion, and fall behind the goal you had set for yourself. I just liked that image.
>
> —Stephanie Hill, Owner of Lightbulb Moment Consulting

> As an immigrant who moved here from China in my late twenties, I often find myself a bit delayed on the path of traditionally defined success compared to others in my age group. Then I reflect on the new language I've mastered, the new culture and art that provide me a different perspective to see the world; a different lifestyle and value system; new friends and colleagues who share their lives with kindness and generosity. This means so much more than traditional success! I'm so grateful for the opportunity *not* to climb a ladder. Follow your heart, not a well-traveled path!
>
> —Lily Angelocci, Transformational Healthcare Lead at UC San Diego Health

Building relationships and creating community is a must for a leader and business owner. I have two mastermind groups that I am part of with women who are in the continuous improvement space and one in the leadership and equity space. Both have been life-changing. That community stretches to individual relationships with other entrepreneurs from all over the world. I could not do life without those essential connections, and I look to build and add more community daily. I encourage everyone to find multiple individuals and groups that feed them and that they can also give to. I mentor and have a group for that as well. These groups sustain and support me when I am on a high or need support in staying encouraged. Community is life-changing and is necessary for all of us.

—Kim Crowder, Certified in Diversity, Equity, and Lean Six Sigma Leadership, and CEO & Founder of Kim Crowder Consulting

REFLECTIONS

Although the emotion that most frequently follows comparison is pessimism, there is a positive side. Our impulse to "compare and despair" reveals our innate connection to other humans, which is a good thing. On that same note, surrounding yourself with people who make you want to become a better version of you, could inspire you to contribute in ways you hadn't considered. What's key is recognizing that you are not alone in your inclination to compare yourself to others. Allow yourself some grace in that awareness.

INK MAKES YOU THINK

- Who are you comparing yourself to and where do you think you fall short?

- What might you ask that person to find out what comparisons leave *them* feeling less than?
- What do you think they'd say?

Consider connecting with that person and finding out. Could be a humorous exchange.

44

DO THE THING YOU FEAR

DO IT SCARED.

This is the title of a book by Ruth Soukup, and it's a good rule for how to operate in the world. The golden moments in my life result from following this counsel. One of the scariest moments was performing improv for the first time in my early 30s. Taking a workshop looked like fun—and the instructor was cute. I had zero intention of being on stage in front of strangers.

The eight-week improv workshop culminated in a group performance for friends and family—at least that was the initial plan. My assumption was that, although the instructor *may* have done this with past cohorts, we were a crew of teachers, firemen, and baristas— unexceptional folks. There was no way our motley efforts at humor would ever cut it. Nevermind that the thought of an audience was terrifying, we would simply never be ready.

Weeks later, when the instructor discovered I hadn't invited a single person, he set me straight. "We *will* put on a show, and you *need* to invite people!" After relenting and disclosing the show to a tiny, select few—much to my horror they came. That final night, the nervous energy in the theater could have powered a generator—a funny generator.

Our troupe spent the night of the performance reeling between panic and exhilaration. The audience gave us inputs, we took them in and made *lucky* mistakes as we melded together on stage. We embodied characters, forwarded plots, and invented scenes. People laughed— with gusto, not politely—and we relished every second.

That moment of bravery led to performing mainstage shows and improvised musical comedies with ImprovBoston for many years. That was decades ago, and it was confronting that fear that gave me the courage to quit a decent job and hang out my consulting shingle. After standing in front of total strangers and making stuff up, how hard could anything else be?

"Doing it scared" most Friday and Saturday nights gave me the guts to launch a career. It also taught me how to listen, trust the process, respect my colleagues, experiment, and invent stuff with other humans. That long-ago lesson is always close at hand when confronting uncomfortable situations. It's always worth doing it scared.

Consider those moments on the job when you are unsure how something will turn out so you play it safe. The moments when you wish you could try something but never mention it; the emails unsent, the requests unasked, the risks never taken. Looking back, are your regrets about things you did, or the things you wish you'd done? Life is short, get up and dance.

———

THE WISDOM OF THE CROWD

What techniques do you use to overcome your fear and dive in?

Here are some of the things I find helpful. Hire a coach to push you outside your comfort zone. Share your scary goals with others so they can keep you accountable. Surround yourself with a community of like-minded people who inspire you and believe in you.

—Jessica House, Founder of LightHouse Counseling and Wellness

First off, when you feel those stress chemicals starting to surge, thank your body for doing its part to make you successful. Stress chemicals are wonderful for focus and endurance.

Also, you need to know that the cues your body gives you are identical for excitement and anxiety. So, when you start thinking you're feeling anxious, tell yourself, oh, wait, I'm actually excited!

—Ruth Archer, PhD, Director of Continuous Improvement at Michigan Technological University

> Many years ago, I attended a Dale Carnegie training. One method they taught, that really helps me move forward on execution, is to ask, "What's the worst thing that can happen?" It may not be the approach that works for everyone, but it continues to prove useful for me!

—Mike Osterling, Co-Author of several books including *The Kaizen Event Planner* and *Value Stream Mapping*

REFLECTIONS

One thing to remember is that you're scared by things you care about. And once you care about something, you're generally willing to invest time and effort in doing it right. The next step is to ask yourself exactly what you're worried about—"awfulize" it. Articulating your fears helps outline exactly what you have to address and whether it's surmountable. The trick is to transfer anxiety into motivation. If you do the work, you'll allay your fears. It's energy—it just needs a little direction.

INK MAKES YOU THINK

- What are you scared of doing?
- What are all the things that make you scared?
- What's the worst that could happen?
- Write your reasons down, and then address what you can. Feel the fear, and do it anyway.

45

GIVE YOUR GIFTS TO YOURSELF

THE COBBLER'S CHILDREN HAVE NO SHOES.

THE COBBLER'S CHILDREN HAVE NO SHOES.

This adage was on display early in my career while working at a consulting firm. The firm had assisted with the rebuilding of Japan after World War II. The principals had written books on Just-in-Time Manufacturing, Setup Reduction. They wrote thousands of white papers on standardization, streamlining and the leadership required to make it happen. Yet the internal reality was slightly more chaotic.

It was up to us underlings to figure out each lead consultant's favorite filing method, engagement structure, and standard operating procedures. There were zero standards. Back then, we laughed at the contradictions. How smart could these geniuses be if they couldn't follow their own advice? Imagine my surprise when the proverbial shoe—or lack thereof—ended up on the other foot?

My mother complained to me that she needed a new landline phone. She said hers had stopped recording messages so someone needed to set her up with a new system. I jumped into action, bought her the new handsets, and my husband installed them the same day. Mission accomplished—super fast.

I immediately texted my four sisters that we'd replaced mom's phones and the new ones were installed. We took turns helping her out—always happy to do my part. My oldest sister responded, "Are you sure she needed a new phone? I noticed that she forgets to clear out the answering system so people are unable to leave messages."

"Oh."

I'd just done two things I know *never* to do; jumped to a solution, and assumed "lack of technology" was the problem. I had done *zero* investigation to figure out what was truly hampering my mother. I threw money at the assumed problem, and still had to deal with the real problem, helping my mother keep her inbox cleared out.

The plight of the shoeless cobbler.

My sister is a landscaper by trade, but she's also an ace problem solver. She would never need a reminder to use creativity before cash. She lives that particular continuous improvement adage on a daily basis. As she probably did from an early age, she was reminding me to put my shoes on.

One of the things that happens when you're proficient in your craft is that you invent shortcuts. You may have a tendency to switch to autopilot since you can bank on a career's worth of expertise. You don't need lists for things you tacitly understand. But something's lost. You'd be horrified to hear that your pilot bypassed the preflight checklist because she knew it by heart.

Human memory is fallible, and the risk is too high. You trust doctors and flight personnel not to wing it—are their jobs more important? You deserve your own advice.

———

THE WISDOM OF THE CROWD

When have you been the errant "cobbler"—not applying your gifts to your own benefit?

> I've always struggled with following a standard process. On one hand, shame on me. On the other hand, it gives me empathy with others to understand their barriers to standardization.
>
> —Stephanie Hill, Owner of Lightbulb Moment Consulting

> My favorite lesson around this is discovering I wasn't applying my coaching techniques at home. As parents, we are in 'tell mode' for years while the kids are young. They hear a constant barrage of commands: "Finish

your vegetables, brush your teeth, get ready for bed."
When they became teenagers 'tell mode' no longer
worked. I had to use humble inquiry and have genuine
interest in 'the learner' who was learning about life! It
was a huge lesson and what a difference it made in our
communication.

—Tracy O'Rourke, Co-Author of T*he Problem-Solver's
Toolkit*

I fall into the trap of wanting to be seen as the expert.
Which means too often I don't take my own advice. I
fail to ask questions when I don't know or I'm unsure of
something. It's the fear of looking like I don't know and
therefore will not be respected. This is a great opportunity to reflect and think more deeply on this and really
ensure I am practicing what I preach.

—Sam Morgan, Founder of Illuminate Coaching &
Consulting

REFLECTIONS

You often consider others worthy of your talents, but then neglect
honoring yourself in that same way. Your opportunity is to turn that
thought process around and provide *yourself* with your gifts on a
more regular basis. Take advantage of these "no-shoes" moments
where you can adopt the beginner's mindset. It's a chance to speak to
yourself in the same helpful way you might speak to others.

INK MAKES YOU THINK

- Where are you weak at applying your skills to your own
  work?

- What would you say if you were coaching someone else? Write that down.
- What would it look like to give yourself the attention you deserve?
- How might you respond?

46

DITCH THE SHOE ONCE IT NO LONGER FITS

YOU CAN ADVANCE OR RETREAT FROM ANY POSITION YOU TAKE.

How often do you change your mind? On a small or large scale? When's the last time you reconsidered your actions? You might agonize over decisions, or delay acting until you're convinced a strategy is airtight. You might see the prospect of switching gears as a form of failure—a waste of effort. You should have chosen the right path in the first place. There *is* another way to imagine these moments.

After giving up consulting and teaching mid-career, fate brought me back. Pivoting from the frontlines years ago to build and market online courses brought huge leaps in learning, and imperceptible losses. For one thing, stepping away from face-to-face interactions placed me many removes from the people I was serving. It took returning to my previous career to remember the importance and power of human connection.

There's been so much for me to learn by working directly with people again. Stumbling through the unknown and solving problems together feels electric. Saying yes to new challenges has been gratifying and rewarding. Looking back, leaving consulting wasn't the long-term strategy for me—but it was the right strategy at the time.

It's liberating to operate with the license to change course—switch operating models, update your goals, go after a different job. Of course, doing this by the hour might be exhausting, but using it as a general rule helps deflect the fallacy of "sunk costs." The fact that you already put a ton of time and energy into one choice or direction isn't a good enough reason to restrict your ability to rethink your path.

There's danger in inertia. As per Newton's First Law of Motion, a body at rest will remain at rest unless an outside force acts on it. If you wait for someone else to make a move, what's the loss in terms of your potential? Have you squandered your excitement and drive? When will you have another chance? What if *you* play the part of the outside force?

This happens on a small scale. You stick with an impractical project even after your discoveries prove there's no real need for it. And it happens on a broader scale when you cling to a disheartening career because a new career wouldn't align with your existing resume or degree. Maybe you get another degree, or appreciate that your depth of knowledge in one field gives you unique perspectives in the next.

Whoopi Goldberg was a funeral make-up artist before becoming a comedienne. Pope Francis was a nightclub bouncer. Julia Child worked for Secret Intelligence before writing her first cookbook, and Michael Jordan switched from basketball player, to baseball player, to businessman. Seeing people embrace new directions is inspiring. Everybody loses when you don't listen to yourself.

THE WISDOM OF THE CROWD

What are your rules around changing course?

> "I like to think about how we make decisions or don't make decisions based on how we *think* we are going to feel. But, If you know you can manage anything that comes your way in terms of the emotions created, there is no reason to wait!"
>
> —Dorsey Sherman, MHSA, ACC, and President of Modèle Consulting

> I have a friend who always says it's not possible to know that you aren't on the right path unless you've gone down the wrong one! I give myself permission often. And I give others permission even more often!
>
> —Karyn Ross, Activator and Author of *The Kind Leader*

What's helped me is to change course *if* new information makes a material difference in the new direction, the cost-benefit analysis or switching costs (technical or cultural) is positive and, it just makes sense. Replace concepts of "failure" with notions of learning, growing, adapting. It leads to more grace.

—Mark Halmrast, Director of Old Republic Title

REFLECTIONS

This topic builds the case for a pair of opportune bumper stickers: "No Reason to Wait" and "Don't Believe Every Thought You Have." The concept of not always listening to yourself is a great one, since the propensity for self-limiting talk is ever present. The only way to find out is to walk the path, otherwise you will never know. Walking the path helps you figure out if it's the right one. You can advance or retreat, just keep moving.

INK MAKES YOU THINK

- What change are you considering, but not seriously?
- What would it take to make the change? Write it down.
- What's exciting about it?

Putting it on paper will help you take a more nuanced look at the possibility for change. Think about it.

47

USE HUMOR, IT'S CONTAGIOUS

DO WE TAKE OURSELVES TOO SERIOUSLY? SOLEMNITY CAN BE OVERRATED.

While setting up a workshop years ago with my colleague Joanne, we jockeyed through a teachable moment. We'd been assigned an odd-shaped room with high-backed, large leather chairs. The chairs were luxurious, but made it difficult to imagine a functional setup given the space and number of participants.

Joanne started to describe a way to do it, when I cut her off. "No! I've got it." Rolling the bulky chairs into position while she watched, it became immediately obvious my idea wouldn't work. Joanne stood with her arms crossed not saying a word. "Let's try your idea." Taking her cue, Joanne rearranged the furniture, and her setup was clearly the answer. She raised her eyebrows at me expectantly.

"I was wrong, and you were right." She laughed and asked, "Can I hear that again please?" I repeated, "I was wrong, and you were right." We both doubled over laughing as we finished the room.

Joanne had taught me her "apology technique" a while back. This overt admission of being wrong was how she and her husband combined somewhat mock humility with humor to keep the peace. Potential standoffs ended in laughter. They both knew the drill and kept each other on task with repeat admissions of being wrong.

I got another technique from my midwestern grandmother. She was tiny and liked to quilt. She was a woman of few words, which made everyone pay attention when she spoke. She had a comeback that always confounded listeners. If you disagreed with her, she often responded with, "I've heard what you have to say. And you might be right, but you're not." The end. Hard to argue with a matriarch who uses such stone-cold logic. That's gotten me out of a few standoffs with a few chuckles.

You may have developed similar "outs" with colleagues and friends. As you get to know each other, you get used to spotting and laughing at typical crosshairs. Like Joanne, I developed one with my husband.

On a trip to the supermarket I let him know he had "just passed the entrance." He was momentarily silent as he seemed to drive right past the parking lot.

After a few beats he offered, "I chose the second entrance." He took the next right, we both laughed, and a comeback phrase was born. Whenever I get it in my head to tell him he's wrong, he chooses the second entrance.

We all feel pressure to be perfect, so there's value in allowing yourself to be human. If you can laugh at your own mistakes, and get others to laugh with you, it actually fuels your confidence to move past perceived errors. We all stumble, so poke fun at yourself, and remove the pressure from everyone around you.

———

THE WISDOM OF THE CROWD

How do you use humor to defuse tense situations?

> Humor, used effectively, can be a great equalizer. Used ineffectively ... a great divider. I think instructors who are adept at flexing their 'funny bone' in ways that make people feel comfortable can also use that to make themselves more approachable and human particularly when approaching tough topics.
>
> —Lisa DeNatale, Learning and Development Manager, Ferrotec USA Corporation

> "It depends. Certainly, humor is an effective tool to break the tension and move on. So is just letting go and applying a little stoic mindset. But if the tension is based on something that has consequences, then some-

times the tension is not meant to be broken but must be engaged and embraced."

—Jamie Flinchbaugh, Author of *People Solve Problems*

"I have a lot of 'Crystal-izations' that I use to infuse humor into situations, primarily when I need to call people to the carpet. It has worked well for me. However, I will admit it took years for me to learn the proper tone and tenor in which to make these statements."

—Crystal Y. Davis, Strategy Consultant, Executive Coach, Speaker, and Podcast Host

REFLECTIONS

You don't want to mask or gloss over big issues but, when appropriate, humor can help a team bond. Leaders with a sense of humor are more successful overall, which is worth exploring for those who see it as a weakness. Using humor to deal with speaking the truth can help people hear what you're saying. As you guide those you work with, you've got options for how to call yourself and others to task. There can be kindness in that type of humor. It tells people it's okay, we're human, but we can do better.

INK MAKES YOU THINK

- Think of a time you were in a situation that needed defusing. What could you have said to bring humor and humility to the fore?
- What are some of your own foibles that could benefit from humor and humility?
- What would happen if you laughed at yourself?

48

REFER AUTHORITY AND GROW LEADERS

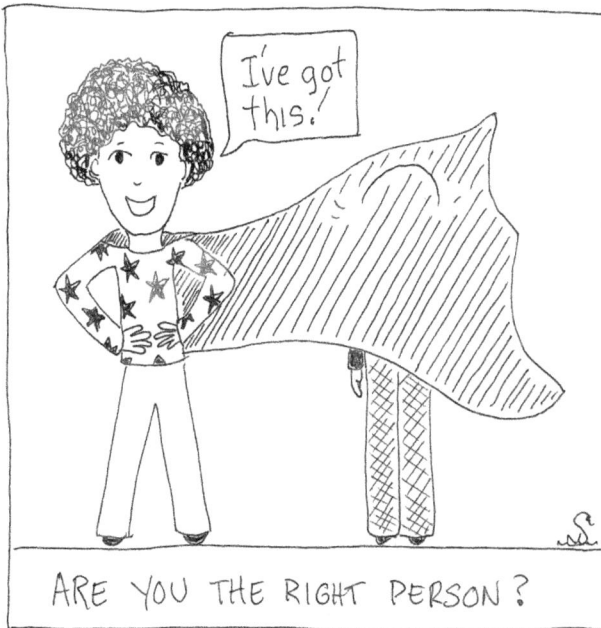

"I'VE GOT THIS."

Those are the confident words of someone taking the helm. But what if taking the helm is a bad thing? Are you the right person? You might be an ace at what you do—better than most—but that doesn't mean you're the only one for the task. What if there's someone else better suited to take something on? Not that they'd be better *at it*—which they may not be—simply better suited.

I find myself doing this in insidious ways. "I'll write that email." "I'll call everyone." "I'll draft that." Sometimes as soon as the words are out, I feel a weight, and realize it didn't have to be me. Luckily, occasionally, someone says, "I've got it." That happened recently with a client and the reality was she needed to be taking the helm. It wouldn't have helped her if I'd taken the lead.

One of the biggest reasons it's hard to resist taking things on is knowing you'd do a better job. Why hand it off if the result would be inferior? That seems bad for business. Or maybe they simply wouldn't do it *your* way. Their work might be up to *a* standard, just not *your* standard. You might be tight on time, and you'd do it faster. Or maybe you take things on out of fear they'd go south without you.

There was an episode of the Mary Tyler Moore Show where Ted Baxter, the iconic newscaster played by Ted Knight, refused to take a vacation. He finally admitted that he was worried people might like his replacement better than him. He feared for his job.

Fear that someone might do a better job is probably the least common reason for not handing off work, but it's one of the reasons. An offshoot is the fear that we may no longer be needed. The workplace is dynamic, and even in the wake of the Great Resignation or Big Quit (the mass exodus of employees after the COVID-19 pandemic), people can still be phased out.

If you see yourself as the only one who can do the task, then how do others learn and grow? An undelegated task may be a missed growth opportunity for someone else. On the flip side, it's a missed leadership opportunity for *you*. If you keep taking things on with that mindset, the burden is heavy. Your workload remains high, which leaves you unavailable.

The answer is something called "referred authority." Stop and ask yourself, "who might be the better person to take this on?" Better in terms of learning, growth, and opportunity to expand the talent in the pool. Consider who that is and hand it off. And don't make it conditional—asking for input and keeping control—truly hand it off. Will people do a worse job than you? Maybe. Will they learn and grow? Yep. Will you reduce your burden? Probably. Will you have time for new challenges? Yes.

It can strangely feel easier to keep piling work on yourself, and it might be a struggle to let it go. Asking, "Am I the right person?" opens a better way forward for everyone.

THE WISDOM OF THE CROWD

How do you keep from taking things on?

> My personal strategy at the start of any engagement is to think about "What does my exit look like? What will "done" mean?"
>
> Will I complete it successfully or will I recommend ending it? When I hand it off to an execution team? What parts of this can I delegate to folks who are closer to the tactical activities or the opportunity? Which of these tasks are a learning opportunity for me? Which tasks are far out of my skill zone and better handled by someone else?

I occasionally get overwhelmed, but it's served me well so far.

—Ramya Venkataraman, Continuous Improvement Leader & Practitioner

When I'm coaching, I ask if they feel they've already absorbed most of the growth and development available from heading the committee, running similar projects, or whatever it is. If so, then they need to let go so they can create space for new opportunities, and let others have the learning opportunity. The people I coach often feel as if asking someone to take over one of their responsibilities is putting a burden on others. I remind them that what's truly happening is they are withholding professional development opportunities from their colleagues and from themselves.

—Ruth Archer, PhD, Director of Continuous Improvement at Michigan Technological University

Even on my own goals planning worksheet, one of the earliest questions is 'who can help me?' And to think sometimes the only cost of getting help is to say 'thank you.'

—Jamie Flinchbaugh, Author of *People Solve Problems*

REFLECTIONS

This is a struggle for many people. You make so many unconscious assumptions that it's critical to take a beat, step back, and ask yourself if there is someone else for the task. Not always easy but it makes you better at guiding those you work with. One mindset that helps is to consider that by keeping the work to yourself, there are opportunities you might be withholding from others, as well as from yourself. "You've got this" is a wonderful thing for someone else to hear.

INK MAKES YOU THINK

- What are you working on that is filling your time?
- Is there anyone else who could take on some of your work?
- What's the worst that could happen?
- How bad would that be?
- What good might come of it?

49

PARTICIPATE! CULTURE IS A CONTACT SPORT

BOILING FROG SYNDROME

THE BOILING FROG SYNDROME, IF YOU'RE UNFAMILIAR WITH THE URBAN MYTH (WHICH FAILS TO HOLD UP TO SCIENCE), IS THE IDEA THAT IF YOU PUT A FROG IN A POT OF BOILING WATER IT WILL INSTANTLY JUMP OUT.

But if you fill the pot with lukewarm water, and you gradually turn up the heat, the frog will stay in the pot until it's cooked. Even if the myth about frogs is wrong, people's willingness to suffer small incidents in silence, hoping things will get better, is a reality. In this scenario, I played the frog.

It happened in an instant but in slow motion, like the boiling frog. During a staff meeting to discuss a recent process glitch, the conversation grew increasingly uncomfortable as the focus of the meeting shifted into condemnation of my colleague. My initial reaction was confusion. When were we going to address the issue of scanning lengthy email trails to find tidbits of information? Shouldn't we be storing information in a central location? The proverbial water was scalding while my mind fixated on our filing system.

My career is ruled by adages such as, "focus on the process, not the person." To quote Dr. Edwards Deming, the Father of Quality, "Ninety-four percent of problems are system-driven and only six percent are people-driven." My mission, for myself and my clients, is to remove fear and create blame-free organizations. I assumed these were obvious facts to everyone in the meeting.

Here was a team leader, a partner of many years, asking our staff to give evidence of my colleague's faults. "She's disorganized. Can you describe your experience of her making mistakes?" It was like an invitation to engage in verbal stoning. The ensuing silence only served to magnify the uncomfortable ambush. But I was frozen—a speechless observer.

Having failed to stand up for her still pains me. Looking back, the water in our culture had been growing steadily hotter for a long time. People knew better, but were too afraid to speak up. It's unclear when it began or why, but I'd been regularly dismissing or rationalizing the warning signs. Things simply needed to return to "normal."

You often fail to recognize the negative shifts in a culture. They can creep up on you, steadily poisoning your environment. You might feel a sense of dis-ease at one moment. You might silently question a decision or a statement at another. Then one day you're shocked to find yourself in hot water, wondering "how did I get here?" Even if the myth about frogs is wrong, people's willingness to suffer small incidents in silence, hoping it will get better, is immense.

Having my own experience makes me more attuned to what's going on in any given group. One thing that helps is surfacing nagging questions. Push for clarity, even if the answers are not things people want to hear. That way, there's a chance to redirect outcomes, or make better decisions if it looks like things aren't going to turn out okay. Clarity drives kindness.

――――

THE WISDOM OF THE CROWD

Have you found yourself in boiling water and, if so, what did you do?

> When we shoot the wounded, people hide their symptoms for self-preservation. The entire organization becomes ill. When we pour resources into strengthening weak systems, people rally to support. The entire organization benefits.
>
> —Michelle Hlywa-Formanczyk, Learning and Development Manager at SA Partners

> To paraphrase Hemingway, 'Things happen gradually then suddenly.' It's the little things we seem to tolerate or dismiss repeatedly. Over time, these seemingly small

unfortunate events get layered on top of each other until they create something much bigger. On the positive side, the same process of little things daily turning into something much bigger applies to the good things in life too!

—Jessica House, Founder of LightHouse Counseling and Wellness

I worked at a super cool company where I was treated like royalty, but my grand welcome was the first red flag. The leadership team had placed inordinate importance on a single hire to save the company. They spent meetings praising me, telling others to be more like me, creating a culture of resentment, unhealthy competition, and demotivation. Very few wanted to work with me. The water felt too warm the moment I got into the pot. I did not stay silent. I spoke with the leaders about how to strengthen the culture but got nowhere. I planned my exit, and left with respect, recommendations, and an acute awareness that not all praise is positive. We should own our strengths, but ensure they are never used against others.

—Sasha Yablonovsky, Revenue Growth Expert, Keynote Speaker, and Co-Ceo of Loanspark

REFLECTIONS

The boiling pot may be fueled by tiny grains of salt. There's the threat of getting burned, but there is a parallel process that results in positive change. The constant efforts by people to tweak and fix the corporate "broth" helps the culture grow and transform. The other thing to remember is that culture consists of not only what you say, but what you *don't* say. Stay mindful of what you're agreeing to. One factor that helps is that with age comes wisdom and a bit more chutzpah ("guts' in Yiddish). If you have to get older—and apparently, you do—it's good to know there are perks.

INK MAKES YOU THINK

- What kind of red flag have you ignored recently?
- What sort of negative behavior have you witnessed and stayed silent?
- What could you say or do about it?
- What is stopping you from speaking up now?

50

ASSUME PERMISSION GRANTED

IS THIS OKAY?

HAVE YOU EVER WONDERED "IS THIS OKAY?" AND INSTEAD OF JUMPING, YOU WAITED.

Waiting turns to inaction and the moment passes. Maybe that turns to regret, and then fades. One thing to consider is whose permission you might be seeking. Have you invented an approval system that no one else knows about?

Something peculiar happens regularly when I put people through a business simulation. The simulation involves a generic process that participants have to run and then improve during successive rounds throughout the day. Everyone has specific roles, and they know what's allowed each round. But knowing those restrictions doesn't stop people from asking if there's any flexibility with the stated rules. Without fail, they check with me to see if they can get some leeway. But that's not what surprises me.

What's unexpected is when participants invent rules that *don't* exist. And they do it every time. They make assumptions about things they aren't "allowed" to do, things no one mentioned. They make up their own restrictions and follow them. Even when I intervene and let them know there's nothing stopping them, they stay in their self-delineated lanes.

That gave me insight on what might stop us from taking initiative. We may have constructed a set of rules in our head to govern our behavior. There's nothing written that stops us, and there may not be anything spoken, but we adhere to the system we've understood. It's unconscious, and it can spread.

A client's boss advised her, "Stop asking for permission and just do it." She said it felt, "Scary but good." It's a liberating message. "Scary but good" is a tantalizing place to be. Typical caveats apply: don't do anything illegal, don't hurt anybody, and so on.

Stop hedging. Own the action. Make it happen.

So often you feel tentative or encumbered. "Can I do this? What will people think?" You assume you need a green light, yet most of the time you don't. The people you defer to may be baffled at the question. There's not even a traffic signal so there's no light to change. Go.

———

THE WISDOM OF THE CROWD

When have you done something without permission?

> My first corporate boss drilled this into my head, "It's easier to ask for forgiveness than permission." There's a line, of course. Get into the driver's seat and stop using the word 'try.'
>
> I lose respect every time. Commit and do!
>
> —Karen Martin, Author of *Clarity First*

> Embarking on my first organizational change was very uncomfortable. I quickly learned the value of embracing the uncomfortable, and making the uncomfortable comfortable. It's all about the journey, not the destination. You need to fall in love with the problem, not the solution.
>
> Be open to pivoting in uncharted waters and be vulnerable enough to ask for help. That allowed me to move forward. At times it was a small step. Other times it was a big leap.
>
> In all cases, I was moving forward.
>
> —Mohamed Saleh, PhD., Founder and Principal at Vizibility

> Regret is powerful, but also easily amplified by 'what ifs' and 'could haves.' When we have an opportunity, a

fear, a chance in front of us, we have to take the leap. Feel it, embrace it, and then take that step anyway.

—Jennifer Lacey, Lean Practice Leader at Robins & Morton

REFLECTIONS

The culture of "asking permission" flows both ways. As you work with others, you may be looking for staff to take initiative, but at the same time you may be keeping a tight rein on the means to do just that. If you insist on doing all the planning and strategizing yourself, people will assume either that you don't need them or that they need your permission. It's this type of bind that leads to hesitation and inaction. Free yourself, and free those looking to you for guidance as well.

INK MAKES YOU THINK

- Where are you hedging?
- Whose permission do you think you need, to do what?
- Do you truly need permission, or is it an assumption?
- How would you find out?

RESPECT YOURSELF—LOOKING BACK

Part Six

Your efforts may go toward shepherding others, but you deserve some of your own counsel. Are you unconsciously sacrificing yourself for the good of the team? Remember the analogy of putting the oxygen mask on first in case of emergency—your selflessness may put others at risk. Being conscious of your mindset is a first step.

Reflect on what you want to modify. You may not be able to change your thought processes, but you can become conscious of them. What do you plan to alter in terms of how you react to them? Will you take advantage of pausing to short-circuit the fight-or-flight response? What aspects of your own advice will you become more mindful of?

KEY POINTS SUMMARY

42. Morph Gaffes into Gems
Plan, but stay ready to ditch the plan.

43. Contend with Yourself Instead of Others

If you spend time worrying about what's happening in other lanes, you'll lose focus of what's ahead.

44. Do the Thing You Fear: Reframe anxiety as excitement and put it to good use.

45. Give Your Gifts to Yourself
You deserve to take advantage of your own advice.

46. Ditch the Shoe Once It No Longer Fits
No decision is final, so move forward and use the experience to make your next choice.

47. Use Humor, It's Contagious
Being able to laugh at yourself, or in general, is an asset.

48. Refer Authority and Grow Leaders
Passing authority to others is not a burden, it confers the honor of leadership.

49. Participate! Culture Is a Contact Sport
Pay attention to signals of a culture in trouble, and act before it's too late.

50. Assume Permission Granted
Consider whether you truly need permission, but either way, don't wait for it.

These lessons are never done. You learn new things as you experiment, and you get a bit better every time. You can revisit the things that make you uncomfortable—the "pebbles in your shoes." What deserves re-examination? What are you good at? What do you want to change? Where should you spend more time in reflection?

REFLECT AND RECONSIDER

REFLECT AND RECONSIDER

What's your picture of yourself now? Are you more aware of your own influence? What kind of leader, colleague, friend, sibling, or parent are you? What kind of leader will you become?

You are older—days have passed since you picked up this book—and wiser. What will you do with all this wisdom?

Have you incorporated new behaviors into your day? Have you started asking new questions? Are you counting to eleven, or at least pausing?

Do you have new questions to pose to those you work with? Have you developed options for guiding people away from rote answers that don't forward the plot? Are you able to hold back from fixing things on your own? Can you provide others with methods to lift their perspectives, and support them in their quest for elegant solutions?

Do you have a better sense of the impact language has on the culture? Acronyms and jargon might shorten an email, but the recipients lose clarity, and a sense of belonging.

Are you able to stay curious and avoid assuming the worst? Every statement and action you take to discover and understand result in less blame, more trust, and a greater willingness of those around you to contribute.

Are you able to set your intentions and use your mornings well? Remember that chasing "in-box-zero" is less important than tapping your creativity when your brain is most forthcoming. Whether it's on paper, or a modern version of paper, write things down since ink makes you think. You're a creature of habit whether you approve of your habits or not—so consider the habits you want.

When you're stuck, do you take a walk, or wash the dishes to conjure your theta waves of idea flow? Use the ingredients your body makes available—like framing anxiety as excitement—and get to work.

Are you able to withhold judgment long enough to write that "sh*tty" first draft? If you can stave off your inner critic, you'll have time to make it better. Do you consider yourself creative? Can you tap into the spirit of your 10-year-old self? The beginner's mind is full of possibilities.

Have you been making time to give others credit? Are you making it easier for those who've failed to recover? It helps to see people's humanity along with their ability to complete their work. When you pay attention to your community, leadership becomes easier. When you put time into relationships, people are more likely to follow you.

Have you cleared away any self-created roadblocks? There will always be someone who could do it better, faster, cheaper, and that's no reason *not* to do it. Have you tried to "do it scared?" Have you switched directions?

Remember, for good or ill, and whether you realize or not, you're a role model. Others are watching what you do and say.

Show them a picture of a leader.

GRATITUDE

Writing a book is a bit of a paradox. It can be intensely lonely, but the collaboration turns it into a party. It's more companionable and goes well beyond appetizers and small talk.

Choosing who to invite, finding out what they brought to the party, and how much they enjoyed dancing. Having "partied" with these people over the past year, I count them as friends. Without their generosity, I would not have lasted the night. I look forward to coming to their shindigs. I'd like to thank all the honored guests who made this book possible.

To My Business Partner

Tracy, you've been the wacky yin to my yang. The only woman who makes me seem like an introvert when she enters the room. You are all heart, purpose, and brilliant dedication. Your simple observations always uncover the humanity of a subject. I've been honored to go through the mire with you, and I look forward to working with you to bring more of our dazzling selves to the world.

To My Book Team

Stephanie Feger, I was so lucky to find you. You've forever changed my journey. You've been an advisor, an advocate, and a fearless defender of deadlines. Each call with you is a masterclass in invention. Your brain is a hotbed of ideas. You told me to "run, don't skip" and luckily, I listened. Thank you, friend.

Sandy Wiles, you worked behind the scenes to help showcase what I brought to the table as an author. You shaped the book's website with creativity and perseverance. You went the extra mile, and I will be forever grateful to you.

Madelyn Copperwaite, I am so glad it was you who crafted my cover. It's tough to capture the essence of a book in a single image, and you did! My eternal gratitude for blending so much of the spirit of the book into a compelling visual.

To my copy editor Brian Manning. Your emails are compact riots. Your writing is so ingenious that I had to conduct a preemptive "Manning Edit." You made me realize I wasn't crazy. If the book made sense to you (and made you laugh) then I knew it had legs. Thanks so much for taking the time, offering your considerable skill, being frank, and being kind.

To My Editorial Board

As my husband can attest, I like a big party, and this impressive clan is no exception. With the rough cut of the text assembled, I opened the door and welcomed in colleagues and friends. Although I don't recommend this technique for parties in general, I'll address them in alphabetical order. Big, heartfelt thanks to Hugh Alley, Katie Anderson, Bella Englebach, Gemma Jones, Karen Martin, Pete Pande, and Jeff & Sally Toister. I salute you all.

Activators and Influencers

Thank you to my friends and colleagues who lit the way for this book. Another awesome party including Mark Graban, Maria Grzynka, Stephanie Hill, Karyn Ross, Dorsey Sherman, and Deondra Wardelle—how lucky to be drawn into your orbit.

To My Clients

Bringing consultants onboard takes a bit of faith. I'm grateful you all took a chance on embracing change with me. You can see the fruits of our work in these pages. The journey is never a straight one, and it's always worth facing the challenges, working toward operational excellence, and cultivating strong, resilient problem-solving cultures. I'm honored we've been able to learn from each other.

To The LinkedIn Community

The pages of this book showcase your generous additions to every conversation. I learned new techniques from you. I heard about books and authors that expanded my education. I benefited from differing perspectives and approaches to our common challenges. You shared your personal experiences, and your examples added depth and breadth to each chapter. It's been a joy to collaborate with you.

To the Women In Lean—Our Table

Thanks to founders Karyn Ross, Crystal Davis, and Dorsey Sherman for igniting a female festival of collaboration and encouragement. My community increased a thousand-fold because of this online nation of boldness and kindness. So many of the contributors to this book came from this collective. I am looking forward to more invention and crucial contributions from this dedicated band of women. We've only just begun. Look out.

To My Friends & Family

You've buoyed me up and made life joyous regardless of the weather. You're good company. Thanks for laughing at my jokes and saying "yes" when it counts. More of that!

GLOSSARY

5S: 5S is a workplace organization method focused on increasing efficiency, reducing waste, and improving overall performance. The result is a workspace that's easy to navigate. It originated in manufacturing but has been adopted in service industries and used in the digital realm. The term 5S refers to a five-step method:

- Sort: Separate what's needed for the workspace from what's non-essential.
- Set-in-Order: Arrange tools, materials, supplies, and equipment, and use labels so everything is obvious and easy to access.
- Shine: Clean the workspace including equipment, tools, and equipment, to improve the overall appearance, open pathways, and increase efficiency.
- Standardize: Establish procedures that outline the plan for ongoing maintenance of the workspace. This includes elements such as roles, cleaning schedules, ordering instructions, and other ongoing standards.

- Sustain: Make the improvements a part of the organizational culture by continuously monitoring and improving workspace.

5 Whys: The 5 Whys is a problem-solving technique used to dig to the root cause of a problem by repeatedly asking why. Once a problem solver identifies an issue, they ask why the problem occurred. The answer to the first "why" becomes the basis for the next question, and so on, until they've uncovered the root cause of the problem. It may not take five whys to get to the root cause or it may take more than five. The intent is to dig past symptoms or surface issues so problem solvers can make lasting improvements as opposed to "band-aid" solutions.

A3: An A3 is a ledger-sized (11x17) document originally developed for use in the Toyota Production System (TPS) to effectively communicate problems, proposed solutions and follow-up plans in a concise way. It's a one-page report that includes visuals to present information that is structured and easily digestible. The purpose of the A3 is to facilitate communication and problem solving within teams to support continuous improvement.

A3 Thinking: A3 Thinking refers to the process of using an A3, a one-page documentation of the problem-solving process. The A3 highlights the problem solvers "thinking" by displaying how they describe the problem, current state of the process, goal, root cause analysis, proposed solutions, and results of implementation. The structured documentation helps everyone involved to quickly communicate with leadership and each other on their progress.

Act/Adjust Step: The Act/Adjust Step of the PDCA (Plan-Do-Check-Act/Adjust) cycle is where the problem solver reacts to the results realized in the Check Step. If they achieved the goal then they work to maintain the new process. If they didn't get the results they wanted, then they plan a new iteration of the PDCA cycle. This is classically where problem solvers make adjustments and refine their approach to the presenting issue.

ADKAR: ADKAR is a stage-gate change management method that stands for Awareness, Desire, Knowledge, Ability, and Reinforcement. Stage gate means you can't progress from one stage to another until you've achieved the goal. An example is not moving on from the "Knowledge" Stage—making sure people know what the change is about—until you've achieved the "Awareness" Stage where people understand why the change is happening. It's a framework for managing change and helping people successfully transition from the current state to a desired future state.

Agile: The Agile method is a project management and product development approach that involves customer collaboration, flexible response to change, and delivering work in product increments. Agile was originally designed for software development but has been adopted in other industries. The approach is based on the Agile Manifesto, a set of values and principles that prioritize customer satisfaction, collaboration, and delivering work in frequent increments. It is typically implemented using "Scrum," Kanban, or a hybrid of both, which involve specific practices such as daily standup meetings, sprint planning, and retrospectives. The method values real-time response to fluctuating customer needs and market conditions.

Analyze Phase: The Analyze phase of the DMAIC (Define, Measure, Analyze, Improve, Control) process in Six Sigma is where problem solvers examine the process and interpret the data collected in the Measure phase, with the goal of digging to the root causes of a problem. This phase involves using process maps alongside data analysis tools to understand the relationships between influencing factors and the problem, and developing hypotheses to test. The goal is to narrow down and determine the critical few variables to address in order to resolve the problem. Those elements become the focus of the Improve phase.

Check Step: The Check Step of the PDCA (Plan-Do-Check-Act/Adjust) cycle involves evaluating the results of the experimentation that took place during the Do step. The problem solver determines if their countermeasure(s) achieved the objectives set out in the Plan Step. Studying the results informs the action plan in the final Act Step.

Continuous Improvement: Continuous improvement is a philosophy with the goal of enhancing the quality of products, services, and processes by making incremental improvements over time. It involves continuously identifying and addressing areas for improvement and making changes that lead to increased efficiency, effectiveness, and customer satisfaction. This is addressed using methods such as Lean and Six Sigma along with employee engagement, data analysis, and regular performance assessments. The goal of continuous improvement is to achieve ongoing improvement and sustained success for the organization.

Control Phase: The Control phase of DMAIC is the final step in the Six Sigma DMAIC method (Define, Measure, Analyze, Improve, Control), where problem solvers create a control plan to sustain the improvements, monitor the process, and adjust the process as needed to ensure continued effectiveness. The Control Phase protects the process from slipping and losing benefits over time, so it's crucial to the success of the project.

Countermeasure: A countermeasure is an action taken to counteract or remove the root cause of a process problem. The word countermeasure is used in the place of the word "solution" to reinforce the idea that it's a temporary experiment and can easily be removed, replaced or adjusted. These are classically introduced in the Do Step of PDCA or the Improve Phase of DMAIC.

Cycle Time Reduction: Cycle time reduction refers to the process of decreasing how much time it takes to complete a process cycle or workflow. This can address how long it takes to create a product, deliver a service, or complete an administrative task. The goal of cycle time reduction is to increase efficiency, productivity, and customer satisfaction. This can be achieved through process improvement, automation, removing steps, reducing inventory levels, and increasing the speed of equipment or machinery.

Daily Standup Meetings: Daily Standup Meetings are short, frequent team meetings where participants stand together while offering quick updates on their work and highlight obstacles they're dealing with. Standing helps keep the meetings to 15 minutes or less, and the goal is to keep everyone informed, aligned, and working together to solve pressing issues. The origins of the format stem from Agile project management, although standup meetings are used regardless of the preferred continuous improvement method.

Define Phase: The Define phase of DMAIC is the first step of the Six Sigma method that stands for Define, Measure, Analyze, Improve and Control. The focus in this phase is on defining the process problem, determining the desired target to achieve, and identifying the stakeholders involved. The goal is to ensure everyone is clear on the issue being addressed and what's expected of all involved.

DEI: DEI stands for Diversity, Equity, and Inclusion. The goal of DEI efforts is to create supportive environments where people from diverse backgrounds are valued, respected, and able to thrive in the workplace. Some goals include diversity in hiring and promotions, creating a culture of inclusivity, and addressing systemic barriers to equality and fairness. The ultimate objective is to build a more equitable and just society where everyone has equal opportunities to succeed.

DMAIC: DMAIC is an acronym that stands for Define, Measure, Analyze, Improve, and Control. It's a five-step, data-driven method used in the Six Sigma process improvement approach. The goal is to identify and eliminate defects in a process, and create value for customers. DMAIC provides a structured and systematic framework for problem solving and continuous improvement in an organization.

- Define: Define the process issue to be addressed.

- Measure: Establish the baseline, severity, and frequency of the problem.
- Analyze: Study the process and the data to determine the root causes of the problem.
- Improve: Develop solutions to address the root causes and implement them.
- Control: Adjust the solutions as needed and continue monitoring the process to make sure the process participants are able to maintain the gains.

Do Step: The Do Step of the PDCA (Plan-Do-Check-Act/Adjust) cycle involves identifying countermeasures (temporary solutions) to counteract root causes, developing a plan to implement them, and executing on the plan. Problem solvers study the results of the experiments in the Check Step.

Gemba: Gemba is a Japanese word that translates to "the real place." It's the physical location where work is happening. "Going to Gemba" highlights the importance of observing a process firsthand, whether it's a physical place or digital workflow. Going directly into the workspace is the best way to identify and remove waste from processes.

Gemba (Process) Walk: A Gemba Walk is an approach used in Lean and other continuous improvement methods to observe and understand processes. Gemba is a Japanese term that translates to "the real place"—the place where value is being created for customers.

The walk involves a problem solver physically moving through the workplace to observe processes, talk to employees, and gather data. The goal is to build a better understanding of how the work is performed and where there are opportunities for improvement. By observing processes first-hand, it's possible to gain insights that wouldn't be apparent from behind a desk or in a conference room. The goal is to use those discoveries to improve efficiency, reduce waste, and increase customer satisfaction.

Hansei: Hansei is a Japanese term that refers to the process of reflecting on one's actions and learning from mistakes. It is an important aspect of continuous improvement and helps problem solvers and organizations identify areas for improvement and make changes that lead to better performance and results. The goal of this reflection is to foster a culture of continuous learning where individuals and organizations are committed to constantly seeking out opportunities for improvement and making changes to achieve their goals.

Improv: Improv refers to the art form of improvisational theater, where performers work together to create unscripted scenes, characters, and dialogues on the spot, in response to suggestions from the audience. Improv is generally performed in front of a live audience, and relies on collaboration, quick thinking, and strong communication skills among the performers. Improv has its roots in theater and comedy, but is also used for educational purposes.

Improve Phase: The Improve phase of DMAIC (Define, Measure, Analyze, Improve, Control) is the fourth step in the Six Sigma process improvement method. This phase focuses on identifying and implementing solutions to eliminate the root causes of the problem identified in the Analyze phase. The goal is to make changes to the process that reduce variability and ensure that the process consistently delivers what the customer wants. Improving the process sets the stage for the Control Phase to ensure that the improvements are sustained.

Just-in-Time Manufacturing: Just-in-time (JIT) manufacturing is a production strategy where raw materials, components, or finished products are manufactured and delivered as close as possible to the time they are actually needed in the production process, reducing the amount of inventory held in stock. Just-in-Time Manufacturing aims to minimize waste and improve efficiency by only producing what is required, when it is required.

Kaizen (Rapid Improvement) Event: Kaizen is a Japanese word that translates to "good change" and a Kaizen Event is a short-term, focused improvement workshop that can span a single day or several days. The goal is to identify and focus on a specific issue or pressing problem that needs to be addressed to eliminate waste within an organization. These workshops are typically led by a cross-functional team of employees who work together to identify root causes of problems, develop and implement improvements, and create a plan for sustaining the gains.

Kanban Board: A Kanban Board is a visual management tool used to display the flow of work and to manage the process of continuous improvement. It was originally developed as part of the Toyota Production System and is widely used in Lean and Agile approaches. "Kanban" is a Japanese term that translates to "signboard."

A Kanban board typically consists of columns, each representing a stage in the process, and cards or sticky notes that represent work items. Typical columns are titled, "To Do," "Doing," and "Done." Tasks are moved from left to right as they progress through the process, allowing team members to see the status of each item and to identify bottlenecks or areas for improvement. The use of a Kanban board helps to balance demand with capacity and ensures that work is pulled through the process only when there is capacity to handle it, reducing the risk of overburdening team members and leading to increased efficiency.

Kata: Kata is a Japanese word that means pattern or standard or practice. The word is commonly heard in the context of martial arts, where kata are the movement patterns practiced by learners to build muscle memory. The objective is not to perfect the particular pattern, but to embed the movements so deeply that they can be brought to bear when needed in a match. (If you've seen the movie Karate Kid, that's what the kid was doing as he waxed the car and painted the wall. If you've ever done drills as part of a sports practice, it's the same concept. The drills aren't the objective; the underlying skills are.) The Toyota Kata are thinking patterns that are repeated by learners so the thinking processes they engender are embedded in the thinking of the learner, and which can then be drawn upon as needed, regardless of the situation. The Toyota Kata supports the concept of learning by doing. In the context of continuous improvement, Kata is often used to refer to Toyota Kata.

Lagging Indicator: Lagging indicators give you the results of things that have already happened, as opposed to leading indicators, which give you some idea of what's to come. An example of a lagging indicator is the percent of patients readmitted for the same ailment they were originally treated for. In contrast, a leading indicator might be the number of patients who received instruction on preventive measures before leaving the healthcare facility.

Lean: The Lean method is a systematic approach to continuous improvement focusing on maximizing customer value while minimizing waste. It originated in the manufacturing industry and was developed based on the Toyota Production System. The Lean approach utilizes the PDCA cycle and emphasizes continuous improvement and the elimination of waste in processes, products, and services. The approach employs techniques such as value-stream mapping, kanban systems, visual management, and standard work. The goal of Lean is to create a culture of efficiency and innovation, where employees at all levels are empowered to identify and eliminate waste and improve processes.

Measure Phase: The Measure phase of DMAIC (Define, Measure, Analyze, Improve, Control) is the second step in the Six Sigma problem-solving method. In this phase, problem solvers quantify the current performance of the process in order to establish a baseline. Determining the current state of the process provides a foundation for the subsequent Analyze, Improve, and Control phases.

Operational Excellence: Operational Excellence refers to a management philosophy and approach focused on maximizing efficiency, effectiveness, and profitability in business operations. It involves the continuous improvement of processes, systems, and technologies to meet or exceed customer expectations. This approach is often synonymous with Lean, Six Sigma, and other process improvement approaches, along with supportive leadership, employee engagement, and a structured approach to improve all areas of operation.

PDCA: PDCA stands for Plan-Do-Check-Act/Adjust and is a continuous improvement cycle that is a part of the Lean method. The PDCA cycle is a four-step process for continuously improving a process or product:

- Plan: Identify a process issue, study the current state and determine the root causes of the issue.
- Do: Develop and implement the plan to experiment with ways to counteract the root cause.
- Check: Study and assess the results of the experiments.
- Act/Adjust: Based on the results of the experiments, either document the new process, or plan to conduct another PDCA cycle to address things like a different root cause or try a new experiment.

Plan Step: The Plan Step of the PDCA (Plan-Do-Check-Act/Adjust) cycle is the first step in the Lean continuous improvement process. This step generally takes as much time and the last 3 steps. The Plan Phase contains the following steps:

- Define the process issue to address.
- Study the process and data to establish the current state of the process.
- Set the goals and objectives for the effort.
- Conduct root cause analysis for the gap between the current state and the goal.

Process (Gemba) Walk: A Process Walk is used in Lean and other continuous improvement methods to observe and understand processes. It's also referred to as a Gemba Walk, where Gemba is

Japanese and translates to "the real place," where value is being created for customers.

The walk involves a problem solver physically moving through the workplace to observe processes, talk to employees, and gather data. The goal is to build a better understanding of how the work is performed, and where there are opportunities for improvement. By observing processes first-hand, it's possible to gain insights that wouldn't be apparent from behind a desk or in a conference room. The goal is to use those discoveries to improve efficiency, reduce waste, and increase customer satisfaction.

Rapid Improvement (Kaizen) Event : A Rapid Improvement Event is a short-term, focused improvement workshop. The goal is to identify and focus on a specific issue or pressing problem that needs to be addressed to eliminate waste within an organization. These workshops, which can span a day or more, are typically led by a cross-functional team of employees who work together to identify root causes of problems, develop and implement improvements, and create a plan for sustaining the gains.

Rework Loop: A rework loop is the process of continuously repeating work due to mistakes or defects in a previous step of a workflow. A rework loop means a process or product has to be redone because it wasn't done right the first time. This happens when the upstream process is flawed. Rework loops can cost money, time, and lead to decreased efficiency and productivity. Organizations use continuous improvement methods to reduce or remove the root causes of rework loops.

Service Level Agreement: A Service Level Agreement (SLA) is an agreement between a service provider and a customer that specifies the quality and availability of services the provider is required to offer. They outline the responsibilities of both parties and the remedies available if the service provider fails to meet the agreed-upon standards. Service Level Agreements are commonly used in business and technology to ensure that customers receive the quality of service they expect and to minimize disputes.

Sensei: In the context of Lean, a sensei is a mentor or teacher who guides problem solvers in the application of Lean and scientific thinking. The term comes from Japanese martial arts, where a sensei is a highly skilled and experienced teacher. The role of a Lean sensei is to coach, facilitate, and support individuals and organizations.

Set-Up Reduction: Set-up reduction is a Lean Manufacturing technique aimed at reducing the time and effort required to switch a production process from creating one product to creating another. The goal is to minimize downtime and maximize production efficiency by streamlining the changeover process. This is a continuous improvement method that studies which tasks can be completed while a process is in operation, which ones require the process to stop, and how to convert more of the tasks into ones that can be done while the process is operational.

SLA: SLA stands for Service Level Agreement which is an agreement between a service provider and a customer that specifies the quality and availability of services the provider is required to offer. They outline the responsibilities of both parties and the remedies available if the service provider fails to meet the agreed-upon standards. Service Level Agreements are commonly used in business and technology to ensure that customers receive the quality of service they expect and to minimize disputes.

Six Sigma: The Six Sigma method is a data-driven continuous improvement approach seeking to minimize defects, improve process efficiency, and satisfy customer expectations. It was developed by Motorola in the 1980s and is now widely used in various industries. Six Sigma involves statistical analysis to identify and eliminate the root causes of defects and process variability. The method uses the problem-solving process known as the DMAIC (Define, Measure, Analyze, Improve, Control).

SOPs: SOP stands for Standard Operating Procedures, which are detailed, written instructions outlining the steps to follow to correctly perform a specific task. They are often in the form of reference manuals to enforce uniformity and consistency in achieving desired outcomes. Standard Operating Procedures often remain the norm once they've been set down. They're used across a broad swath of industries to ensure quality, safety, and efficiency in operations.

Standard Operating Procedures: Standard Operating Procedures or SOPs are detailed, written instructions outlining the steps to follow to correctly perform a specific task. They are often in the form of reference manuals to enforce uniformity and consistency in achieving desired outcomes. Standard Operating Procedures often remain the norm once they've been set down. They're used across a broad swath of industries to ensure quality, safety, and efficiency in operations.

Standard Work: Standard Work refers to a detailed, documented procedure for performing a specific task or process that outlines the current best way to carry out the work. It helps to ensure consistent quality, reduce waste, and increase efficiency by providing clear instructions for performing each task along with why each step is necessary. Using Standard Work provides a baseline for continuous improvement and helps managers both train people and determine whether or not people are following the standard. Standard Work is designed to be updated as new and better practices are discovered.

Takt Time: Takt Time refers to the pace at which a product must be produced to meet customer demand. "Takt" is German for a beat or pulse in music. It's a way of determining the optimal "drumbeat" for a process. It's calculated by dividing the total available work time by the number of units or services that have to be completed during that time. The result is the unit of time that each unit or service should be exiting the process.

Toyota Kata: Toyota Kata is a teaching approach used by managers, supervisors and team leaders to generate adaptiveness, improvement and innovation—through the practice of scientific thinking. It encourages a methodical and systematic approach to reaching challenging goals. Practicing the Toyota Kata routines makes anyone and any team better at navigating uncertainty and achieving challenging goals. Toyota Kata does not teach problem solving, but rather a mindset and way of reacting that makes people more effective at problem solving. The two main elements of Toyota Kata are a practical scientific pattern, called the Improvement Kata, and an associated set of simple Starter Kata practice routines for both the learner and the coach. Practicing these routines helps make the scientific-thinking patterns, and how to teach them, habitual. It is the result of research that posed the question, how can we teach people the thinking pattern that is inherent in how Toyota develops solutions?

Training Within Industry (TWI): Training Within Industry is a management training program developed by the U.S. government during World War II to improve industrial productivity. It consists of four training modules designed to address specific managerial challenges: Job Instruction, Job Relations, Job Methods, and Program Development. The goal is to help managers and supervisors improve their leadership and communication skills, develop efficient processes, and foster a positive workplace culture. TWI is still used by many organizations as a means of improving productivity, quality, and employee engagement.

Voice of the Customer: The Voice of the Customer (VOC) refers to the input and feedback from customers about their needs, wants, and expectations of products and services. It's a critical element in continuous improvement efforts because it provides improvement teams with insights about what customers value, what they are looking for, and what they perceive as quality. It's gathered using surveys, focus groups, customer interviews, and direct observation of customer behavior. By listening to and incorporating the voice of customers, organizations can improve customer satisfaction, increase customer loyalty, and enhance their overall competitiveness.

VUCA: VUCA stands for Volatility, Uncertainty, Complexity, and Ambiguity, and refers to the unpredictability and instability that organizations and individuals face in today's world. VUCA describes the rapidly changing business environment and the need for organizations to be nimble and adaptable to succeed. Part of the challenge is managing risk and ambiguity to make decisions in an environment of constant change.

Wiki: A wiki is a website that allows its users to create and edit web pages collaboratively, typically without the control of a central authority. The term "wiki" comes from the Hawaiian word "wiki wiki," meaning "quick." One of the most commonly known wikis is Wikipedia, the online encyclopedia that anyone can edit. Many organizations create their own wikis to provide background and customized information related to the company.

INDEX

DO-IT-YOURSELF INDEX

What's this?

This is where you capture the things that matter to *you*. A standard index—invaluable—is just that, standard. You've got the opportunity to craft a bespoke collection of resources, quotes, and techniques you'd like to access when you want. I've provided you with some standards such as, "Quotes to Repeat" and "Books to Read."

Design your own reference pages based on what matters to you, and you'll always know where to find them. Now that you know you can write in your books, it's a great way to retain and recall what you read.

Ink, as you know, makes you think.

DO-IT-YOURSELF INDEX

DO-IT-YOURSELF INDEX

DO-IT-YOURSELF INDEX

DO-IT-YOURSELF INDEX

WHAT'S NEXT?

Are you inspired?

Is your picture of yourself coming into sharper focus? The secret sauce for lifelong learning is constant experimentation. You can advance or retreat from any position you take. My improv mentor, Kevin Shone of ImprovBoston and The Groundlings, taught me the rule of three. When you experiment with something new, try it three times before you decide whether it works or not. You're improvising too, and each attempt gives you useful information so you can adjust your approach. Resist dismissing an intangible tweak until you've given it a chance.

You can come back to the lessons in this book whenever you recognize a stumbling block. You'll approach each story with new eyes every time you visit. Different voices from the crowd will resonate, and you'll have new answers for the prompts within "Ink Makes You Think." Consider it a perpetual resource.

NEXT STEPS WITH ELISABETH

Speaking, Coaching, and Workshops

Are you looking for more? Allow me to bring these micro-lessons and more into your organization. Connect with me if you're interested in having me come speak, run customized workshops, or coach you and the people you work with. Building strong cultures means growing good problem solvers and cultivating leaders that people want to follow.

Check elisabethswan.com and JITCafe.com for the latest speaking, coaching, and workshop offerings.

Bulk Book Orders

Provide each team member with personal and professional development opportunities by giving them the gift of *Picture Yourself a Leader*. They can learn and experiment on their own, or you can work with them to guide their journeys. Bulk discounts are available to underpin your team's growth and education.

LET'S STAY IN TOUCH

BLOGS AND NEWSLETTERS

Are you interested in receiving the latest stories and lessons from the field? Say yes! Sign up at: elisabethswan.com.

LEADERSHIP ASSESSMENT

Would you like to assess yourself as a leader? Take the quick, free online assessment at: Elisabethswan.com.

LEARN MORE AND GET IN CONTACT

Elisabeth@elisabethswan.com | ElisabethSwan.com

FIND, FOLLOW, AND SHARE ON SOCIAL MEDIA

LinkedIn.com/in/elisabethswan
Twitter.com/consultswan

ABOUT ELISABETH

"Elisabeth Swan can zip, button, and sew." This was the headline in a newsletter created by my 12-year-old neighbor. He had access to a mimeograph machine so the catchy one-pager made a splash on the street. My mother still quotes it, and I can verify being adept at all three of those skills. Read on for more formal biographical bites, and of course, the best bits come at the end.[1]

Elisabeth Swan is an Entrepreneur, Consultant, Instructor, and Coach with thirty-plus years of experience helping people identify and resolve barriers to operational excellence. She works across an enormous span of corporations, hospitals, universities, and nonprofits—helping people cultivate problem-solving cultures with less friction and more engagement.

Her background in improv and storytelling has forged her unique, inviting approach to work and life in a field that can suffer from unintentional barriers. Onsite or online, she's found that people learn faster and embrace change more freely when the content is interactive and packaged with average humans in mind.

In 2018 she co-authored the hugely popular, *The Problem-Solver's Toolkit: A Surprisingly Simple Guide to Your Lean Six Sigma Journey*. She has worked with hundreds of clients and her experience includes efforts such as co-designing and leading the global Lean Six Sigma rollout at Starwood Hotels and Resorts, coaching the leaders of a local child-care nonprofit to become Lean Six Sigma Green Belts, and designing interactive, online problem-solving workshops for the University of Denver.

As a Managing Partner of GoLeanSixSigma.com she codesigned the highest-rated online Lean Six Sigma training and certification available. As Co-Founder of the Just-in-Time Cafe she co-hosts a regular podcast and invites industry luminaries to present free monthly webinars with the driving belief that a rising tide lifts all boats.

Other milestones that influenced her journey? She performed for years with ImprovBoston—perfecting the five-act, completely improvised musical. She won the Ultimate Frisbee National Championship with her team, Lady Godiva, in 1988, and she wrote the following limerick:

This book has all the best words
Packed with adjectives, nouns, and adverbs
Oddly compelling
With top-notch spelling
Nirvana for sentency nerds

𝕏 in a

---

1. Props to Michael Bungay Stanier, author of *The Coaching Habit*, for paving a new way to describe an author.

www.ingramcontent.com/pod-product-compliance
Lightning Source LLC
Chambersburg PA
CBHW052015030426
42335CB00026B/3149